MW01168846

THE MARKETING MD

What Still Works To Attract New Patients.
Plus What To Do When You Run Out Of Ideas.
+
Delivering the right message, to the right patient,
at the right time, makes every patient,
the best patient.

By Michael Tetreault

Elite MD, Inc. | Elite MD Publishing
4080 McGinnis Ferry Road
Building 800, Suite 801
Alpharetta, GA 30005

DEDICATION

**I lovingly dedicate this book to Catherine Sykes,
Dr. Melton, Dr. Buddy Crum and Mrs. Nielson,
my 8th grade English Teacher.**

Catherine Sykes,
You've taught me so much, personally, spiritually and professionally. You allowed me to: make mistakes, graciously made them teaching moments; provided environments for free thinking to create businesses; shape industries; design and write books with you that are now changing people's careers … Thank you! I am what I am today because of you. I'm forever grateful.

Dr. Melton,
Years ago, you allowed me the privilege to write for you and "sort of" started paying me for it. ☺ Thank you for believing in me way back when and guiding me to where I am today.

Dr. Buddy Crum,
On whose shoulders I have been privileged to stand and learn so many things about the business of business. It was in our countless early morning meetings that I caught a glimpse of what could be and should be for my life. Thank you for being a great teacher.

Mrs. Nielson,
You kneeled down next to my desk one ordinary afternoon in Layton, Utah. You encouraged me to continue writing and believed in my talent way back when. That one moment is forever engraved in my heart. Thank you.

Michael freely provided direction and much needed assistance when I left my job to open up a solo concierge [medical] practice. He encouraged me to remain independent and build a practice as unique as I am. In so doing, I am 16 months in and will never look back.

~Osteopathic Doctor (DO) | Connecticut

"Your book was very helpful and even led me to a webinar which was great! And even though this whole business aspect of medicine is a little overwhelming, your resources have been keeping me sane and actually excited about what my future in medicine may be.
Thanks for what you and your staff do.
Continue the good work!"

~Family Physician | Paramus, New Jersey

"Michael has one of the most creative brains I've run across in my 30+ years in business! He is thoughtful and brings not only creativity but a solid research and business acumen to the table."

~Executive Director | Marketplace Alliance Group

TABLE of CONTENTS

Introduction | 11

Chapter 1 | You Must Pay To Play. | 25
Chapter 2 | Move With A Plan. | 35
Chapter 3 | Being A Tortoise Is Fine. | 55
Chapter 4 | Consumer Confidence. | 65
Chapter 5 | Million Dollar Question. | 73
Chapter 6 | Return On Effort. | 103
Chapter 7 | Going Digital. | 133
Chapter 8 | Handling Social Media | 147
                  & Your Online Reputation

BONUS MATERIALS | 165
What To Do When You Run Out Of Ideas.

❖ Merry Marketing: 4 Fun Holiday Promotions

❖ Top Performing List Companies To Help Your Medical Practice Grow In Any Economy.

❖ The Top 50 Web Site Design Resources.

❖ When To Use Billboard Advertising

8

"I was working at a large academic medical center with many physicians who each took shifts covering the entire patient population. I realized quickly that when I was not the physician on call, my patients had to discuss their issues with whoever was available that evening or weekend. I was constantly coming back to find changed treatment plans and confused patients. This disjointedness broke the intimacy and personal relationship that you develop with your patients over time. I eventually just stopped using the call service altogether and gave my patients my personal phone number so they could call me instead of someone they'd never seen before. That was when I realized I needed to practice medicine in a different type of setting so I could truly give my patients the best possible care."

Dr. J.B. | Physician | Omaha, NE | July 2013

INTRODUCTION

The Coming Storm.

The Affordable Care Act (ACA), Medicare Cuts, declining insurance reimbursements, and the shortage of primary care doctors – this is bad news for those in healthcare right now. Today, the marketplace is competitive and patients are looking for faster, cheaper alternatives outside of health insurance plans that don't pay you what they used to. With the advent to the World Wide Web, consumers (i.e. prospective patients) are using the Internet to become more aware and informed of the doctors available in their area, the cost, a physician's background and they can even read and write about a doctor's reputation.

Over the years, I find that most people who purchase or download my books usually fall into one of two categories, possibly a third. First and most common, a doctor who is on a rescue mission to save his/her medical practice from closing its doors. He or she is yearning to learn and find solutions to a growing problem ailing more and more medical practitioners across the U.S. This person is usually open to new ideas and needs information, direction and advice on how to acquire new patients so they can keep moving forward. Notice I say, keep moving forward. On any rescue mission, no matter how bad it gets, you must keep moving forward.

The second category of readers that are attracted to my books are those with a dream. Physicians and healthcare practitioners with big ideas and goals they eagerly want to accomplish. This person also shares a desire to learn. Steven Covey writes in his book, *The 7 Habits of Highly Effective People* ... "If I really want to improve my situation, I can work on the one thing over which I have control - myself." Nothing could describe better those people who have dreams and are moving forward towards them.

The third and most uncommon category is the healthcare practitioner who bought 'just another business and marketing book' and is looking for a golden nugget or two for which they can apply to their particular situation.

I'm hopeful anyone who is reading this book falls into one of those categories and will feel like the time they've spent with me was worth the price of the book and some positive feedback on Amazon.com. But I caution you, if you bought this book thinking 'it has the magic formula for marketing and attracting new patients' or you read the words ... 'this is the proven system', that's not what the next several chapters are about.

As you well know, the path to obtaining, attracting and marketing to patients has changed for healthcare practitioners today. Years ago you could fill an internal medicine or family medical clinic simply by joining one two good HMO or PPO plans in your area. Physicians simply didn't need marketing because the large insurers and managed care network directories were good enough and essentially filled these healthcare practitioners clinics until they were busting at the seams.

Fifteen years ago, the Medicare Fee Schedule was seen as the bottom of the barrel in managed care network negotiations. Today, MCO networks are seeing 75% and 80% of Medicare contracts arrive on their desk. The unfortunate part is, all too many healthcare practitioners are shaking their head and reluctantly agreeing to these fees because they see no alternative to finding a steadier stream of patients. Combine these distressing facts with the anticipated Medicare cuts, and it's no wonder why so many doctors are retiring, selling out to hospitals, choosing to start a cash-only clinic, go into concierge medicine or direct pay care or opting to retire altogether.

The know-how and how-to's of harnessing the power to get new patients on-demand is what many doctors and medical practice staff have dreamed of for years. But it's no easy task. There isn't a clear road map or one-size fits all approach to growing a medical practice. Over the years, I've advised and helped hundreds of healthcare practitioners across the U.S. in the areas of family medicine, primary care, chiropractic, dermatology and many others specialties and one thing is certain, everybody's practice is different and requires a varied strategy in specific geographic areas to successfully acquire new patients and grow a medical practice with the least amount of cost and frustration possible. There is a road map, but it's one that is learned and there are map keys that you need to know that will help you accelerate your efforts. Meaning, once you know how the map

√

works, you can shorten the time you spend to get to each destination or goal you have for the future of your practice and business.

It takes time to study a map and find where your destination begins and ends. Learning what will work on your map will take a lot of time and some designated amount of money. This comes with the territory of owning any business. What I've seen, heard and learned is that way to many doctors don't know where their marketing map is let alone how to navigate their marketing plan, promotional message or digital reputation. They have no compass that's guiding them. Where's true north on your map when at the end of the year you've spent more money on administrative typing tasks to submit insurance claims than to get your name out in your local community to tell people about how great of a doctor you are? I've seen it all. I've seen annual expenditure sheets and tax statement with $2,000 of marketing expenses and $138,000 spent in administrative overhead. Worse yet, I've seen no money allotted in past years for any marketing.

"Maybe we should be examining why our patients would rather go to a retail clinic that see us (their primary care doctors)," said Dr. Robert Nelson, a direct primary care physician in Cumming, GA, a suburb of Atlanta, GA. *"Here are just a few of the comments I hear from PCP [primary care physician] patients as to why they come to the retail care centers instead of their primary care physician: my PCP doctor couldn't get me in; my PCP doesn't do stitches anymore; my PCP doesn't do x-rays in office; my PCP doesn't take walk-in patients; my PCP usually refers me to specialist for everything anyway; and my won't return my calls. Instead of viewing the status quo PCP model as the center of the universe, maybe we should take some plays from the Retail Clinic playbook before we become obsolete."*

Dr. Robert Nelson in Cumming, GA
www.mydocpps.com

Retail Medicine Does A Good Job Of Marketing.

The business of medicine has changed and a few savvy physicians are recognizing they have to change too. Physicians are become better typists than they are better doctors. Retail medicine, urgent care centers and doc-in-a-box clinics are swallowing up market share with easier appointments, transparent prices and faster service. No longer are we in an age where a physician can grow and support a medical practice by simply relying on an "in-network" status with most of the state-wide HMO and PPO plans across the country.

Retail medicine and price transparency are quite possibly the future of affordable health care in the U.S. Like most large pharmacies, the creators of 'Retail Medicine' understood years ago the need marketing affordable, convenient and price-driven access to healthcare – and soon, they'll be serving the masses.

"Until retail and concierge medicine came along, we would blindly walk into a doctor's office or hospital and not know (or in many cases, care) about how much things cost," says Catherine Sykes, Managing Director of *Concierge Medicine Today*. "We don't purchase our homes, our vehicles or other services in this way. It's time we stop using our health insurance card as a form of credit."

Price Transparency Is The Future.

Get Used To It. Retail medicine, doc-in-the-box clinics, they're the next competitor to medical practices across America.

A lot of modern health care medical centers and physicians across the U.S. are now starting to show their prices to their patients before they sit down for a visit. Dermatology offices and direct primary care clinics are a good example. Until recently, hospitals, primary care and other health care specialties were one of the only segments in the U.S. that rarely listed how much their fees were for their time, services and products.

"Maybe we should be examining why our patients would rather go to a retail clinic that see us (their primary care doctors)," said Dr. Rob Nelson, a direct primary care physician in Cumming, GA, a suburb of Atlanta, GA. "Here are just a few of the comments I hear from PCP [primary care physician] patients as to why they come to the retail care centers instead of their primary care physician: my PCP doctor couldn't get me in; my PCP doesn't do stitches anymore; my PCP doesn't do x-rays in office; my PCP doesn't take walk-in patients; my PCP usually refers me to specialist for everything anyway; and my won't return my calls."

There Is Hope.

Fortunately, every field in business except for most of those in healthcare office have perfected marketing channels and strategies to acquire new customers (i.e.

1

prospective new patients) and it's simply a matter of learning, editing and mastering your marketing map in your practice to make this dream become a reality. There's no such thing as an overnight success and mailing out a postcard once isn't going to cut it. If you stay on the path to average, which is where most traditional, managed care and insurance centered doctor's offices spend their time and money, you'll become one of those medical centers or clinics that eventually says 'marketing doesn't work for me.' Do you think Bill Gates, Steve Jobs, Jay Parkinson, MD or Jeff Bezos would every say that?

In the coming chapters, you will learn how to; develop, edit, manage a master your own marketing map. You'll learn what it takes to find, create and use local community events to promote your practice; how to better interact and engage in social media and online and offline marketing activities; foster and encourage more positive patient feedback; analyze, monitor and manage your offline and online reputation using medical profile microsites that take minutes to update; seek physician and patient referrals from your local hospitals, specialist centers and colleagues; and last, what commonalities your marketing map should have that other successful physicians who've travelled down your path have done.

As a bonus, we'll teach you how your web site to not only a place that can generate new patient leads for your practice, but how you can turn them into educated consumers and new patients that know exactly what you offer and what value it will bring to their lives. Finally, this book will accelerate your learning curve so that you know how precisely how to rinse-and-repeat your own marketing process, over and over, for better and faster results as you grow.

"You don't have to be seen everywhere.
You simply need to be seen everywhere
in your niche!"

Doctors using online and offline marketing is now entering the small and mid-sized medical practice in a big way. Marketing and appropriated targeted promotional strategies are literally changing the way healthcare providers engage with their patients, daily, weekly, monthly and throughout the course of an entire patients' lifecycle at a medical practice. These are practices and business tools that many health providers, such as yourself, are probably not accustomed to.

There's a gap between healthcare providers and patients and the valley is only going to wider as the Affordable Care Act is implemented, insurance exchanges are used and physicians work inside hospital systems. Without proven, effective and targeted marketing strategies, the distance will continue to grow. The best way to retain your patients and find new ones is a daunting task. It's best said by a mentor of mine, author, speaker and business trainer, Maritza Parra, 'Become a star in your own backyard!'

As social media, online advertisements and modern smart phone and app technology changes the way all of us interact with each other, attracting, educating and engaging with your patients' needs to be a task you should understand and manage effectively. The writing of this book is to be used to help you do just that.

Whether a patient needs to be sent a text message appointment reminder, a Happy Thanksgiving card through the mail, three appointment reminders over the course of the next six months, or someone wants to opt-into an electronic e-newsletter they found on your web site that you distribute once a quarter containing reliable health education information addressing their specific nutritional or disease concern -- a thorough marketing plan will equip your medical practice with the tools that make it easy to manage the message that's right for your patients, changing forever the patient relationship with you and your practice and enhancing every patient experience.

What To Expect When You're Starting.

We all have great ideas, big dreams and probably some million dollar inventions that someone else not nearly as smart as you developed years later and brought to market. Now their millionaires and you're working in healthcare. You might have thought to yourself, 'I'm way smarter than that guy. I thought of that back in 1991!'

Well, what stopped you from moving forward with that idea, invention or dream? What caused you to say, 'that's just not going to work? It's a waste of time. It'll take too much work.' The answer is, you probably talked yourself out of the idea entirely. You were probably too smart!

The same can be said about need for marketing, public relations and advertising in healthcare. Think about where you are in the business of medicine today. How did you get here? Why are you reading this book? You've probably stumbled or learned about this book because you're in a learning phase in your business or life. As Jon Acuff writes in his book *Start: Punch Fear in the Face, Escape Average and Do Work that Matters,* as people in our careers, we must go through three very distinct stages or phases in life to become masters of our business. Nothing cripples your business, budget or causes more frustration that spending money and not seeing results, right? Marketing and the success that follows is learned, edited and thereafter, mastered.

To know what to expect before you start, you must understand that marketing is strategic, eventual and a gradual process that begins with learning … baby steps, if you will. When you decided to be a doctor, you went to school to learn. This probably happened in your 20's or maybe into your early 30's. You were in a learning phase. Next, you graduated, applied your learning and as your expertise, personal bedside manner evolved, you adapted to your patient's needs, chose those tasks and services that you were really passionate about and fine-tuned your practice and place in medicine. This phase probably occurred in your 40's or possibly even in your 50's. And now, you're in your 60's. Colleagues are coming to you asking you for advice and they're taking you to lunch and want to know 'how'd you do it?' at the local coffee.

Wouldn't it be great if we could just skip all of the years of education, learning and school loan debt that accompanied the learning phase in our career? What if we skipped out on all of those years you had to perfect your craft, visit patients in the hospital or treat someone before they passed away in the privacy of their own home surrounded by friends, family and loved ones.

Very rarely will the mastery of marketing find you by accident. We all search for shortcuts. We all secretly hope there is a backdoor to our dream. But there's not. When confronted with work or reward, more often than not, we'd choose reward, me included. But the secret to marketing is that there is no secret. It's an unlocked door. You simply need to open the door and learn, edit and master the map.

CHAPTER 1

You Must Pay To Play.

'You mean I have to spend more money?' This is a common statement I hear more often when talking about marketing with healthcare practitioners. If we can overcome the financial challenges and emotional barriers to spending money before we begin on marketing and help your practice grow as fast and cost effectively as possible is why we're here in the first place. I understand better than most that nothing is more frustrating than spending money and not seeing results. It's happened to me. But think of it this way, spending money on advertising and marketing is similar to making financial investments in safe decisions. You advertising and marketing dollars drive new business and help you reach the growth you deserve and need – but you have to feed and water your plant(s) to make them grow.

The second secret of marketing is it doesn't happen by accident. Now that you're free to start down to the path to learning, you might be tempted to take the shortcut to mastery. Don't. Don't be tempted to spend marketing budget money without a plan or apply your own learned knowledge to the promotion at-hand.

Most people already have a reference for TV, radio and print costs but not so much for online marketing. U.S Bancorp's Piper Jaffray conducted an interesting breakdown of the estimated average cost of acquiring a new customer. Combining this research with McKinsey and Company's estimates, the calculated price-tag for each new customer looks like this:

- $230 per customer thru Television Advertising
- $125 per customer thru Specialty Magazines
- $70 per customer thru Direct Mail Campaigns
- $20 per customer thru Print (E.g. Yellow Page Advertising)
- $8.50 per customer thru Internet (E.g. SEO)

Are you considering purchasing email lists? While I don't necessarily recommend this approach, some marketing professionals do agree that purchasing a local area list of email addresses that fits your particular medical practice demographic audience is a good idea. If you're considering this option, you should at least know how much these lists costs ... and that's what I'm going to share with you before you begin.

- 50,000 emails – approx. $80-$100
- 100,000 emails – approx. $120-$140
- 500,000 emails – approx. $250-$300
- One Million emails – approx. $450-$900

Should I Hire Someone Internally Or Pay A Company?

"Really competent advertisers have a better handle on the pulse of the culture than anybody else," notes Rush

Limbaugh in a recent discussion about SuperBowl advertising in January 2014 on his syndicated radio show. "It's their job. They have one job: Separate people from their money willingly. Their job is to convince John Q. Public to give up his money for whatever they convince John Q. Public he wants."

He continues to say, "I've always believed that if a company hires an agency to sell its product -- to market and sell its product -- that agency has to know the culture. That agency has to know cool, it has to know hip, and it has to be able to predict it, and it has to be able to personify it.

It has to be able to hire people who are it, or who recognize it, who can write it, who can produce it in TV commercials. There's all kinds of different advertising. There's cost per thousand, there's results oriented, there's impressions, any number of ways of going about it. Television advertising in the Super Bowl is a combination of cost per thousand reaching eyeballs, but also results oriented and branding.

If you watch the advertising -- actually, in anything, in any prime time show. For example, prime time, you watch any show that's targeting the 25-54 demographic, and you will learn what those people think is cool, hip, and where our culture is. So if you watch the Super Bowl and really take time to watch the commercials and study 'em rather than be entertained by 'em, you will find out you'll have a pretty good bead on where the country is culturally.

√

How to improve
your health
over 55

The 55-plus hasn't been abandoned, but the advertising aimed at them is simply aimed at maintaining brand loyalty and establishing that the products they love are still good and still work and maybe are being improved. But you will not see advertising aimed at those people that's designed to get them to switch brands. The advertising aimed at 25-54 is all about that. And, by the way, not every advertising agency knows what it's doing. That's why some are better than others. It's like any other business, some Super Bowl commercials, you say, "What the hell was that?" Utter failure, if that's your reaction."

Don't get this confused with what a 'marketing consultant' or 'marketing company' is. These are two very different types of consultants. A Marketing Consultant should have marketplace expertise in both writing and designing materials and effective, lead-generating communication for your practice. They're usually individuals that a medical practice will hire and bring into the practice internally as an employee.

Marketing agencies or ad agencies typically offer both offline and online advertising strategies to grow your patient-base and be able to outline a plan that works with your budget. They are typically paid by the project or will quote you prices for the services that you wish they perform.

Which one is better? Well, physicians and healthcare practices over the years tell us that budgeting money and giving it to a marketing agency or ad firm is the most effective strategy of growing a medical practice. More often than not, the internal marketing person or employee you've hired will naturally take on daily tasks and duties put onto them by the doctor or staff that is not part of their job description. Overtime, staff find that a marketing person or "employee" of a medical practice is not as effective as they'd hope they would be because they're paying a salary to this person plus, marketing and promotional task expenses.

'If you build it they will come ...'
is a strategy that worked for a corn farmer in Iowa,
but that's not the real world we live in.

Patient Referrals Is All I Need.

What a lie. Most of the time when I hear doctors say they don't need marketing because they have a full practice due strictly to patient referrals, they're typically speaking to a microphone and a panel of marketing experts in a crowded room so they're colleagues in the audience will know how great they are. Yet, this doctor is still attending a marketing conference. Why would you attend a marketing conference if you don't need marketing or receive all of your patients by referral? Are you lying to yourself or do you actually belong to enough HMO and PPO panels that you've come to believe that you're practice is growing based on patient referrals? I'm not saying it can't happen, but it's rare – I mean, really, really rare.

Well, anyway, I digress. We talk to doctors every day who are looking for sound marketing advice and just won't take it. We tell them 'if you believed patient referrals was all you needed to grow, you wouldn't need to be calling me.' I also hear this … 'if we just do a fantastic job of treating our current patients, we never need to 'do' marketing.'

There are two things wrong with that statement. First, you don't just 'do' marketing. That's like firing a pellet gun from a thousand yards away to hit a buffalo. 'Doing' marketing is about learning your audience, developing a plan, implementing the plan and sticking to the plan. Sure, you may make some navigational changes along the way, but slow and steady always wins the race.

The second thing that is foundationally wrong with that statement is there is no such thing as the perfect practice whereby all new financial growth is amassed by referrals. If you build it, they WILL NOT Come. Sure, 'if you build it they will come …' is a strategy that worked for a corn farmer in Iowa, but that's not the world we live in. Our practice is located on Main Street USA … yeah, you know the one!

According to interviews over the past five years with hundreds of doctors and healthcare staff, the number one most successful way they attracted new patients to their practice was by … 'hiring a marketing agency' to help with the educational component of your practice. Why? Because the practice hadn't learned, edited or mastered marketing. They mastered the treatment of chronic and acute illnesses and prescription refills. But, when interviewing and talking to "successful" medical practices (those earning $300,000 annually and above per year), they understood that it was more important to hire someone who had acquired a mastery in the field of marketing.

EMAIL ADDRESS

MARKETING TIP #423!

If you ask patients for e-mail addresses in order to provide them with special offers or for patient referral bonuses -- this type of marketing costs you considerably less than having to advertise and market for a new patient in your local newspaper or networking event.

CHAPTER 2

Move With A Plan.

The importance of a marketing plan cannot be overstated. It's the map by which you will navigate the dollars spent and activities and growth you need in the months ahead. So many doctors and medical clinics carry on day to day without this critical piece of a business. Would you even think about opening a medical practice without a phone system or bank account? Would you spend thousands of dollars on a web site, postcards and graphic design and not know how and where in the coming months you will use these tools to generate new patients? Think about it: there aren't many things in life that you would get into without a plan. Marketing is no different. Your overall marketing plan should cover about a six to twelve month period, and it should be made up of monthly, if not weekly to-do' tasks and timelines.

This Is How You Do It …
Figure out how much money is in your budget.

As we all know, marketing of any kind costs money. How much money you are willing to commit to the cause is going to determine some key factors about how that money can be best spent. We talked about this in Chapter 1. Following those successful medical practices who've ventured before us, they tell us you should allow somewhere between 3% to 8% of your annual budget each year for specific marketing tasks before we begin.

Remember, you want to be economical but you also need to be realistic on what it will take to pull in the leads you need to close new and repeat business.

Determine your target market.

Who is most likely to walk into your practice each week, like your bedside/exam room manner, trust your treatment(s) and buy your services? Are they married? Are they executives? What is their income level? Do they have children that will visit my practice? These are the kind of questions you need to ask yourself, your staff and your patients in the form of surveys.

One of the most common mistakes in marketing a medical practice, or any business for that matter is … answering "Everyone" to the question "Who is your target market?" It may be that you have more than one target market, but there is no product or service in the world that appeals to each and every person. Even Pepsi and Coca-Cola target different people with their messages.

Any marketing professional worth their salt will be able to identify your specific target audience based on a number of local geographical data elements, meaning, if you give them a little time, they'll tell you!

Typically, educated and established patients in primary care, family medicine, dermatology, dental and chiropractic care fall into this category:

- Well-Educated, Obtained at least one College Degree per household.
- 61% Female (Note: Most females and Mothers are the healthcare CEO for their family and decide who their family and children will visit)
- 71% Age 35+
- 66% Household Income of $60k+
- 52% Caregivers to children or other family/relatives
- 90% seek to be well-informed about drugs before using medication.
- 5 xs – Five times more likely to visit an online pharmacy than average population.

Food For Thought.

Even though it's been established by the healthcare community as well as ad agencies, that people older than 55 years of age have all the money, they also have everything they need and want, or at least most of what they want. They've established over time their brand loyalty. The difficult challenge for doctors and those assisting healthcare providers market and grow their practice is understanding that it would simply cost too much to get them to change their minds. That's why you start studying marketing principles and begin really analyzing other practices who are successful and you'll see that most healthcare marketing is aimed at people in their thirties, forties and fifties.

I'm not saying this is your specific target audience. You should learn your target audience and every community is difference. Hiring a marketing consultant or PR/Marketing Firm will accomplish this rather quickly and effectively. However, if you're unfamiliar with what the most common and 'ideal' patient demographic looks like for most healthcare clinics, these are the common traits and characteristics you will find become loyal patients to a medical practice and deliver the best patient referrals.

You are the one, once you've analyzed the data that must decide who is MOST LIKELY to buy what you have to sell and target that prospective patient audience. Your message to Moms will be different than your message to businessmen even if the product is exactly the same. Different city communities may require different mail pieces or advertisements.

Use the Right Vendors, Mail Houses, Graphics, Etc.

In making sure that your message is getting across to the right people – prospective patients who are in the market for what you're offering - it usually comes down to finding the right mailing list. Typically, for medical practices and 99.9% of all healthcare offices, patients will live and/or work within 3 to 5 miles of your practice. Knowing this, you find a zip code map of your city, put a pin where your practice is and draw a circle approximately 3 to 5 miles around your practice. This will tell you the zip codes you should target for purchase.

There is a great deal to know about mailing lists.

There are pointers you should follow when buying a zip code mailing list that tell you what to watch for in a mailing list company to make sure they're reputable. They are:

Get references. Talk to other people that have purchased mailing lists from that company. If you don't know, Google their name and read reviews. Read past page 1 or 2 of Google and you might be surprised how much information you will find.

Do they guarantee on delivery? That means due to the inevitable number of bad addresses there are in a list, can they still guarantee a high percentage of deliverable addresses. That number should be 90% or better. People move all the time so a mailing list company cannot guarantee 100% deliverability - but they should guarantee at least 90%.

How often do they update their information? Do they include recently moved to the area addresses also from the last quarter? They should be able to answer this question and should be updating their information monthly.

You can get burnt on mailing lists - it is the most expensive part of your marketing plan due to graphic design, postage and printing costs. Ask friends who own businesses, whether in the medical area or not. Don't just purchase from the first person that tries to sell you mailing lists. Remember, don't be impulsive. Do your research.

Select several media (3-5) outlets in which to promote your practice. (i.e., Direct Mail, PPC, Press Releases, etc.)

Being A Tortoise Is Fine. But one size, one thing or one selecting only one marketing outlet is never the best approach. You might think, 'all I can afford is a web site right now.' Well, the decisions you make right now before you implement your marketing plan will determine the future growth of your practice for the next 6 to 12 months. You beautiful part is, you have so many affordable options now a days and prices are constantly coming down on PPC (pay-per-click) ads, web site design, brochures, business cards, postcards, vinyl banners, etc. If you have not done a good deal of marketing in the past we recommend picking three media outlets to start. This is much easier to keep track of and you will better be able to track return on investment (ROI) and return on effort (ROE).

Category Options And Promotional Outlets Available To Doctors:

- **Internal/Inside The Practice**
- Offer Bottled Water In Office Lobby
- Place Telephone In Rear of Office – not near front desk. (No one waiting in your lobby wants to hear your staff leaving messages)
- Offer Coffee Throughout the Winter Months.

- Offer Lemonade During The Hottest Summer Months.
- Provide Indiv. Wrapped Snack Items (i.e. Bars; Cookies; Etc.)
- **Updated Male/Female Reading Materials** – It's recommended not to have ANY magazines from the former month. Groupon has plenty of affordable magazine subscriptions to help save you money and keep your waiting area/lobby up-to-date with the latest issues.
- Nothing is more irritating to patients that an **On-Hold System** that will not allow you to speak to a live person. Successfully physicians review their telephone system needs twice per year.
- **Screensavers --** In-Office Ads/Signage/Promo that you personally create (or your staff) in the form of JPG images made into screensavers are incredibly effective. Design some for your exam rooms if you have a computer in the room and have them rotate every 10-20 seconds. It's easy, free and a nice personal touch that will keep your patients informed, educated and updated on the latest news and information in your practice.

Digital Marketing Categories

Update your Web Site. Be certain to include on your homepage a Lead-Generation form, allowing the visitor to give you their email address directly on the Homepage. Your landing page (also sometimes called a "squeeze" page) is a web page whose sole purpose is to capture a lead. As you may remember, this is a form of "pull marketing" designed to pre-qualify a visitor prior to them visiting your practice. The theory being "pull marketing" versus "push marketing" is that you are "pulling" them towards your products/services when they need them. Therefore, if someone does not enter their name and email for a free related offer then chances are they will not part with their credit card details at your practice either.

Whether you're selling primary care services on one site (or domain) and your blogging on another site, your website is probably the first place you will be able to attract the attention or make an offer to a prospective patient who is searching for the services you offer. By definition, a landing page is just what it sounds like: it's the page your website visitors arrive at after clicking on a link they found by using a popular Internet search engine. It could be your home page, or any other page in your site. Generally speaking, 99.9% of private-pay physicians as well as those traditional managed care-style physicians are used to being found in insurance directories and receiving patient referrals. That's hamster-wheel medical marketing and today we're in B2C marketing.

That being said, all medical practices now need to consider their messaging, colors, layout and offers as part of a new way of creating a steady flow of patients. As one physician recently said, 'Instead of viewing the status quo PCP model as the center of the universe, maybe we should take some plays from the Retail Clinic playbook before we become obsolete.'

Text Message Appointment Reminders (SMS) – Physicians across the country are finding appointment reminder services that work well with your existing EMR/EHR platform and can extract your existing patient contact information to communicate regularly via SMS Text Message with patients. Appointment bookings are up, missed appointments are a thing of the past and you're in control of the messages you want to send. HIPAA laws have recently changed as of October 2013 so be sure you get permission from your patients before you begin an SMS Text message campaign. Talk with your local SMS Text Message and appointment reminder vendor such as www.SolutionReach.com – companies like this one should be up-to-date on the current procedures and be able to help you.

PPC Advertising (Pay-Per-Click) on Facebook and Google – Physicians recommend spending a minimum of $10/day or $150 per month. Your choice.

SEO/Backlinks – The purpose of Backlinks is to get your website showing up as high as possible when your patients (and prospective patients) are searching for your practice on a search engine. A "backlink" is a term that refers to links that point to your websites or webpage from another website. There are several ways that backlinks can be created. All of them may help increase a site's traffic, simply because Internet users will have more opportunities to click on links to the site, but not all types of backlinks will improve a site's search engine ranking. This is because most search engines will evaluate the "quality" of the backlink based on things such as the popularity and nature of the site from which it originates. For example, a backlink about your medical practice from a website that blogs about auto parts will provide no "quality" SEO value and is unlikely to improve a site's search engine ranking. But, a backlink about your practice on a medically related website could significantly improve your SEO ranking.

High-quality backlinks for your practice from industry-affiliated websites can be purchased by some marketing companies, but you need to be careful and cautious about what "they" consider high-quality and make sure they're industry-affiliated. All-in-all, Backlinks increase the overall search-ability and "quality" score of your medical practice web site on the search engines.

Online References, Links and Digital Citations - WHY ARE THEY IMPORTANT? An example of an Online "Citation" might be an online yellow pages directory (of which there are many) where your business is listed, but not linked to. It could also be a local chamber of commerce or a local business association where your business information can be found, even if they are not linking at all to your website. There are now hundreds of places online where your practice citation can be listed and it is currently not.

44

Another very important point related to references and citations is that businesses with the greatest number of citations may rank higher than businesses with fewer citations. Citations from well-established and well-indexed portals (like Superpages.com for example) help increase the degree of certainty the search engines have about your business's contact information and categorization. To paraphrase former Arizona Cardinals' Coach, Dennis Green, citations help search engines confirm that businesses "are who we thought they were!" Citations are particularly important in competitive niches (like primary care) where many service providers don't have websites themselves -- or they have poorly designed web sites. Without much other information, the search engines rely heavily on whatever information they can find.

Mobile Web Site – There are free and paid services that will convert your current web site into a mobile friendly web site. Because more and more people are accessing web sites on tablets, iPads and smart phone devices, you don't want to be behind the curve when it comes to allowing a patient to read about your medical practice on one of these devices. Mobile Friendly web site templates might include: www.dudamobile.com; www.zoho.com; www.conduit.com; www.mobilizedtoday.com and others.

Online Reputation Management and Online Review Monitoring on Microsite Profiles – This is SO important and a component that may doctors and office staff can manage, update and utilize to market their practice with just a little time. Listing sites such as:

Vitals.com; HealthyGrades.com; ZocDoc.com; GetListed.org; EverydayHealth.org; RateMDs.com; DrScore.com; Switchboard.com; Yahoo.com; Bing.com; Google Local; YP.com; Kudzu.com and AngiesList.com allows searchers (i.e. prospective patients) to narrow their search by categories of services and view past patient reviews.

It would make sense to take the time to monitor monthly these comments, tie your services to as many of these categories as possible so that your business appears in more instances when a person is searching. Most are free. Some require a subscription.

Pandora Ad(s) – Incredibly effective sites one physician in Florida and very affordable, this can be a very targeted and cost effective way to promote your medical practice to a target demographic of your choosing.

Encourage Online Reviews From Your Patients Before They Leave The Office – Did you know that most online patient reviews rate doctors highly, seriously, it's true. In a world increasingly dominated by social media, doctors are becoming more concerned about managing their online reputations. Some doctors have even resorted to making their patients sign a gag order before treatment. Despite all the controversy, medical professionals need not fear online reviews: sites like

Yahoo! Local and Insider Pages show that the majority of patients rate their doctors 5 out of 5.

Rather than asking patients to sign a gag order, perhaps doctors should be asking their patients to fill out online reviews — chances are, you'll get top marks. Unsurprisingly, people commonly complained about rudeness, billing hassles, and long wait times. Regardless of how much people value medical expertise, customer service is still important.

Cardiologists, for example, were repeatedly credited for saving their patients' lives and oncologists were frequently described as compassionate. Chiropractors, for all the flak that they get from the healthcare community, received the highest average rating (4.61 out of 5) of all health care specialists, while endocrinologists got the lowest rating (a mildly positive 3.56 out of 5 — maybe the patients didn't like to be repeatedly told to modify their diets), according to DocSpot.com.

Vitals.com for example, is the destination for more than 100 million patients each year who need to find a new primary care, specialty or ancillary doctor, prepare for a visit or schedule an appointment. Their target audience is impressive too: Female – 65% women, the household health managers; Affluent – 33% have a HHI over $100,000; and Educated – 66% have a college education.

Other MicroSite profile listing sites to help you manage online reviews and your reputation online include: Vitals.com; HealthyGrades.com; ZocDoc.com;

GetListed.org; DocSpot.com; EverydayHealth.org; RateMDs.com; DrScore.com; Switchboard.com, Yahoo!, Bing, Google Local, YP.com, Kudzu.com and AngiesList.com allows searchers (i.e. prospective patients) to narrow their search by categories of services and view past patient reviews.

It would make sense to take the time to monitor monthly these comments, tie your services to as many of these categories as possible so that your business appears in more instances when a person is searching. Most of these sites are free. Some require a subscription.

With just a little bit of effort and a quick reminder before your patients leave the office, 'don't forget to leave us a review online!' … you can make a big difference. Start using them today!

Since repetition is the key to marketing success, using three media outlets to begin with will help you reach the same people multiple times. If you run a local magazine or HOA ad in a neighborhood near your practice and send out a postcard, you run the risk of the majority of the people only seeing your ad once. It's better to stagger the release of these items and choose one different outlet each month. However, if you send out the postcard twice in one quarter, you can guarantee that you get your message to the same people twice and you will start to build that know, like and trust factor we talked about earlier in the Value Ladder.

Once you are seeing the returns from your selections or if you decide that one is not working for you, you can branch out into another form of advertising. Over time you will build up a very diverse set of media tools inside your marketing plan.

The percentage of patients likely to recommend a physician to a friend after becoming a fan of their Facebook Page is 56%.

Source: The Direct Primary Care Journal, © 2013

Determine a Schedule and Stick with It …
No Matter What.

Figure out how many people you have in your target market (i.e. zip codes you've determined earlier). For this example we will use Direct Mail Marketing. If you have a mailing list of people in your target market that has 1500 names, figure out how many times per month you can mail a postcard to them and still stay within your monthly budget. Once you come up with this number, do it! Note: you might want to look into bulk-mail houses that do both printing and postage. This can save you a great deal of money over a 6 to 12 month period.

Successful marketing plans set realistic goals. Goals are navigational intersections on your personal marketing map. Every doctor's office marketing map and navigational intersections will and should look different. But when spending money on marketing, and ALL successful medical practices who we've studied do spend a certain dollar amount of percentage on these tasks, you should thoughtfully consider your ROI (return on investment). Doctors must also consider the amount of time and effort put forth internally, graphically, administratively, etc. What I call ROE (return on effort). Analyzing ROI is now more traceable and accessible than ever and I'm not just talking about social media or PPC (Pay Per Click) advertising. If you send out three different postcards, use three different telephone numbers. Then, at the end of the month, look at your telephone records for each number to determine which postcard and promotional message was most successful.

Social media marketing ROI is difficult to measure in terms of direct sales, but can be achieved when time and budgets are set. At the beginning of a social media marketing campaign or program it may be difficult to judge how much time should be spent. Start slow and allocate a specific number of hours necessary to achieve desired results. Only add time when warranted. Social media is not a waste of time, but it can be a tremendous time-waster. You limit your exposure and potential losses by managing time wisely. The investment of time and resources is worth it though – if you've learned what to do and what not to do. According to information published by CrowdSpring.com, 51 percent of Facebook friends and 64 percent of Twitter followers are more likely to buy the brands they follow or are a fan of.

In closing, the importance of having a marketing plan cannot be overstated enough. Create one, follow it and you'll start seeing the benefits – but remember, don't be impulsive. Plan your work, work your plan and adjust any messages quarterly, not monthly.

"Your overall marketing plan should cover about a six to twelve month period, and it should be made up of monthly, if not weekly to-do' tasks and timelines."

CHAPTER 3

Being A Tortoise Is Fine.

There is a lot to learn from those doctors, office managers and other healthcare pioneers who ventured into an uncertain marketplace before you. They've done so standing in your same shoes. They approached each marketing expenditure and navigational direction with caution and optimism. Because we're not big on impulse purchases around here, it's more than okay to take things slow and steady. After all, didn't the tortoise win that race?

Successful People Are Colossal Failures.

As we've talked with hundreds of healthcare practitioners over the years, they'll be the first to tell you they made mistakes. No one marketing plan or business is ever going to be perfect. As my father-in-law likes to say, 'you're allowed to make one mistake a week.' A humorous anecdote, sure, but what if we held ourselves to the truth of that statement? Would we measure up? How many mistakes have you made in business that you now see as learned experiences? They will help you navigate through the same decision next time, right? I know I've learned from my mistakes, many times.

What's critical that we focus on here is that when examining the data from your colleagues, the majority of smart, well-educated doctors and medical practice business owners found that the best and fastest way to grow their business was to hire a marketing firm or Ad/Public Relations company that uses both offline and online marketing strategies to grow their medical practice. This included all of the following ideas shared earlier as well as revisiting your web site, your social media strategy and developing great low-risk offers for your business. We'll discuss the importance of low-risk offers in the chapters ahead.

Take advantage of the Internet, the pharmaceutical and DME representatives that visit your office. They want your business and if you're willing to take a minute to talk to them, they just might share with you what they're seeing out there as they pound the pavement day-after-day. You could potentially learn what NOT to do in your practice.

From 2009 to the writing and recording of this audio series and book, January of 2014, I asked some local medical practice owners what form of marketing they found to work best to grow their practice, acquire new patients and stimulate more positive patient feedback and referrals. The results were as follows:

- 7% use Facebook to grow their business and get new patients.
- 2% use Twitter to grow their business and get new patients.

- 5% use postcards to grow their business and get new patients.
- 5% use a letter alone, to grow their business and get new patients.
- 18% use a letter with a brochure about their business and get new patients.
- 21% say hiring a marketing/PR company that used both online and offline marketing strategies helped grow their business and generate new patients.
- 3% say hiring a business management consultant to organize internal processes grew their business and obtained a few new patients.
- 9% participate in local area networking activities and events.
- 16% say local area advertising combined with low-risk offers helped grow their business; and
- 14% say word of mouth from existing patients helped to grow their business.

Success Story

Interview with Dr. Shira Miller -- Facebook's First Concierge Physician To Reach More Than 10,000+ Followers!

As Concierge Medicine Today (CMT) caught up with Dr. Shira Miller, Founder and Medical Director of The Integrative Center for Health & Wellness, a concierge menopause, post menopause, and anti-aging practice for men and women -- We asked her some important questions pertaining to the topic of social media and marketing a concierge practice online. Topics also covered included her success on Facebook, email and what she does to attract new patients to her practice. Here's what she had to say...

CMT [Editor, Michael]: What tips, tricks, message crafting concepts, etc.; would you give to other [concierge] physicians considering using social media to help attract new patients?

DR. MILLER: I believe that social media is a great way for prospective patients to learn of your existence and get to know your expertise in a non-threatening and non-committed environment. Then, if they like you and trust you and need a doctor like you, they are more likely to choose you.

CMT [Editor, Michael]: Would you suggest only it (i.e. Facebook) for [marketing to] your current patients?

DR. MILLER: No way. My patients get inside info and special treatment that is not available on Facebook. And, the main reason I use FB is to gain exposure and educate people who are not my patients. My current patients already know me and what I do, and I know them, and we have each other's email addresses which allows for most excellent communication. Don't get me wrong, many of my patients are my FB fans and they continue to learn through my updates and help share my information with their friends, but they are the minority. I also use Twitter and LinkedIn.

CMT [Editor, Michael]: Would you encourage the use of email marketing?

DR. MILLER: Yes, email is great. I have a newsletter that goes out about 1-3x/month. I actually think I could use it more effectively and am currently working on that.

CMT [Editor, Michael]: What creative methods have you used "inside" your practice to encourage positive word of mouth?

DR. MILLER: First, I try my hardest to make sure I continuously improve all my patients' health, make them feel great, and give them better customer service than I promised at sign-up. Second, I let them know that I am working hard on building my practice and treasure their referrals. To connect with Dr. Shira Miller on Facebook, go to http://www.facebook.com/menopausedoctor.

What Kind Of Messages Do I Communicate?

Before a patient will walk in your door, most need to know what you're all about, right? They probably think it's important to actually 'like' their doctor and they need to trust your opinion. If you're simply communicating to your local community … 'Here I am, Dr. So-and-So and I'm open for business …' patients are not going to develop a concept of who you are. They need to know, like and trust you first before they will become a long-term, desirable patient for y our practice. It's all about establishing useful and informative communication.

When doctors and their healthcare staff ask us, 'what should be included or communicated in our Value Ladder?', we always tell them you need to be the medical practice that knows about the latest technology, treatment protocols, new applications and is informing people (i.e. your local community) about interesting industry news. You simply can't build your practice, hang a sign on the door and expect people to walk-in. You've got to build that know, like and trust factor – and this is done over time, strategically and methodically. Think drip, drip, drip – but over a period of weeks and months. Remember, there's no magic theory or system that will provide you patients tomorrow. There are only tools and strategies that you can use to accelerate their decision(s) to visit your practice.

How Often Should You Look At Internet SEO And Web Site Reports?

Monthly, Not Weekly and Definitely, Not Daily! We recommend no more than once a month or once a quarter and no more. You'll want to review quarterly and sometimes monthly a comprehensive search engine ranking report (I recommend Google Analytics), that will review your SEO popularity, 'unique' visitors data, keyword search density data, time on site and most popular pages. Remember that lead-generating web site design vs. billboard web sites (i.e. pull marketing vs. push), getting found online and offline and earning a new patients know-like and trust score is a science, not a right. I truly hope this helps. I know it's A LOT to process.

We Take Care Of Our Own.

I love healthcare and I am passionate about the people we help in it. What I love most is that colleagues near and far, at least most, are willing to share their failures, mistakes and successes with others so that we can learn from their past. At some point in your business, a marketing consultant, and salesman or ad agency, may approach you and promise you the world. Maybe you've already bought into their plan and are skeptical of current marketing results they've achieved altogether. It's at this point in time where I remind you that we're in the "Learning" phase of what it takes to be most effective when marketing a medical practice.

The first thing any good marketing consultant or ad agency will do it look at your current competitors in your local, learn and find what's working well and what isn't for them. Gradually, after a few weeks, we'll have learned from those around your practice with the greatest amount of success.

Following these examples helps us accelerate our learning. It helps us navigate the learning curve on the map with further intensity. It means looking at what the men and women around you and in your industry see what exactly they are doing to grow their medical practice and replicate or cease tasks you're currently doing. These great and maybe not-so-great healthcare providers have obviously found some amount success in your local market and have spent a great deal of time and money to get where they are today. Steven Covey writes "...to learn and not to do is really not to learn. To know and not to do is really not to know." — Stephen R. Covey, *The 7 Habits of Highly Effective People: Powerful Lessons in Personal Change*

Who Is Doing Medical Marketing Well?

Answer: Dentists, Dermatologists', Dental Implants.

Dental practices are surprisingly 'doing' web marketing and patient acquisition very well. So are dental implant practices as well as the LASIK eye surgery industry. You can learn a lot by watching and listening to their advertisements. Not only are they similar in fee-for-service business model practices, but they're acquiring new patients and attracting them online very efficiently.

This is important because as you know, retail medicine marketing is where DPC and concierge medical practices are soon going to be pulling their patients from. We should be analyzing and reviewing what dental practices (some, not all) are doing locally to attract patients online and offline.

We've included some examples of sample "Lead-Generating" Web Sites and Matching Facebook Lead Gen Fan pages for your reference. (See:

http://dotcomsecretswebsites.com/lead-generation-samples/)

Wi-Fi Is Now The Equivalent Of Free Refills…It's Expected!

Make Sure It's Free And Readily Available.
In Your Practice.

When was the last time you went to a restaurant and they didn't refill your lemonade or water glass? Probably, pretty rare. Well, free Wi-Fi is becoming the norm (as free refills are to the restaurant industry) in most modern medical practices. Hardly a quarter goes by without the news of skyrocketing smart phone sales and surging numbers involving mobile users accessing the Internet.

Smartphones offer distinct opportunities for your patients to "check-in" to your Facebook Page, (thus a referral to countless friends of that patient in just seconds…hello!). More and more practices are making it easier for patients to take advantage of these features by installing Wireless Routers in their practice. A wireless router can be purchased at any big-box retailer for under a $100. Free Wi-Fi is as simple and easy to implement in your practice and doesn't cost you any additional internet fees (in most areas). to your patients.

"Free Wi-Fi is a no-brainer when thinking of ways to add-value to your patient experience. There's nothing more frustrating than having a waiting room with frustrated patients ... then making those patients pay for their own Internet. Talk to your I.T. contact about setting up a secure Wi-Fi environment at your practice. It costs practically nothing and you're patients will love you for it!"

CHAPTER 4

Building Consumer Confidence.

In every medical practice/business there are always people who will purchase just about anything you are selling, right? You've probably noticed this in your own practice. There are usually a limited number of patients who will most likely buy anything you sell to them. Their perceived value in your and your services matches the price point you're offering.

Then there are those patients who need a little more information and persuasion. This audience is aware of your services, history, reputation, etc., and eventually, they'll purchase something from you -- with just a little extra effort on your part and some patience.

Last, there's always a significant portion of a practice that always wants something for free or deeply discounted. They don't know you or trust you yet...so you've got to build trust with them so that in turn, they'll begin to know, like and trust you in the near future.

Construct A Value Ladder.

The same principle holds true when developing the Value Ladder for your medical practice. You start at the bottom of the scale with a free, low-risk, no-obligation offer. This engages and interrupts your prospective patient audience and qualifies them as part of your next step of the scale. Meaning, if they took advantage of your free-offer, maybe they'll come to our meet-and-greet with the doctor next month?

In an article by Internet Multi-Millionaire Russell Brunson, he states *"You create an irresistible offer to bring someone into your value scale. If your customer receives value from you at that point, they will naturally want to ascend up to be able to receive more value from you."*

Therefore, after a person that you've identified as a prospect begins to walk up your very own business's value scale, you wouldn't immediately try to sell them on an MRI or high-dollar dermatological procedure would you? If the answer is no, you're beginning to understand how the value scale and these principles work together.

So, as you can see, the more perceived value your current patients and prospective patients receive, the higher price point they will be willing to pay. Educational articles and low-risk offers help nurture this a lot. Are patients upset that they have to pay their doctor co-pay or more money after they've received an irresistible offer from you or they've been with you for a couple years? No. They are typically happy that you were able to see their problem and promptly fix it.

Very few unsuccessful medical practices that we have seen have ever diagramed out step-by-step where they are trying to take their prospective patients and current patients after they respond to one of their offers. They normally are so excited to have new patients that they start trying to sell them everything, or worse, they get so nervous that they don't sell them anything.

When you create your Value Ladder, you can predictably know how much money you will make for every person who requests your irresistible offer. You will also know on average how much money you can make from each of these patients and you'll know the lifetime value of those customers.

Remember, all buying decisions go through an evaluation and buying process that will last in healthcare from one month to eighteen months, according to Social Blue Media, 2013. Effective marketing needs to reach your target patient audience every month because you simply do not know at what time each prospective patient will essentially 'buy-into' your practice. In this way, strategic creation of a Value Ladder is essential for long-term success. It's like a B52 airplane rolling down a runway. As your strategy gains momentum, you've eventually got multiple places and people you are dropping subtle messages to about your unique medical practice.

You have probably read articles online or heard stories about businesses that have used companies like Groupon, Loclly and Living Social, and they will get 50, 100 or more customers in a one day or one week. They then complain and say that they lost money by running the offer. Those companies who are complaining are the same companies who haven't thought through their Value Ladder.

Hopefully, by now, you've probably started to see how the Value Ladder works and how these principles are so critical to consider and construct before you move ahead you're your own future marketing activities, correct?

Strategic creation of your Value Ladder from the start and before you send anything out or pay for something just because you 'think' it works … breeds familiarity with your service(s). The more family we are with a service, the more apt we are to walk-in, schedule an appointment, make a phone call or buy something from you. If we don't know about a service, incorporate educational content into your Value Ladder.

Finally, here's a quick tip … consider browsing sites like GroupOn, Loclly or LivingSocial. Look at what offers are selling and those that aren't. These are great places for you to begin thinking strategically about your own Low-Risk/Irresistible Offer.

The Meaning Behind Brand and Company Use of Color

What Color Choice Will Compel the Best Response From Patients?

This is probably the absolute last thing on your mind when it comes to growing your practice. If that's the case, make a photocopy of this section and send it to your graphic designer … they'll appreciate it. But, in the event you are interested in learning how color does play a role in compelling patients to take action, schedule an appointment, give you their email address online or establish you as an expert in your community, there are a few things you should know. Not be taken lightly is color choice, especially when creating graphical elements to your website, fliers, advertisement, brochure, logo, etc., for a medical practice.

Of course everyone has a favorite color, but doctors should be aware of the meanings behind colors, as well as what colors yield the best response from patients.

Red – Known as an attention-getter, the color red draws attention, and is often the color that eyes are drawn to first. It is also known to increase the heart rate and create a sense of urgency, and is often used for clearance sales and to evoke the emotion of 'listen to me – I have something important to say.'

"Of all the hues, reds have the most potency. If there is one electric blue, a dozen reds are so charged. Use them to punctuate white, burn into bronzes, or dynamite black." — Jack Lenor Larsen

Its complimentary color is green according to WebSiteMagazine.com, however, adding just a spot of red can be useful in some cases, because it can accent other colors or draw attention to a specific spot of an advertisement or webpage. Big brands that are associated with the color red include <u>Target</u> and <u>Coca-Cola</u>.

Orange – This is an ambitious color. It is associated with fun and energetic times or citrus fruit. It is recommended for kid's websites or call to action buttons, such as subscribe, buy or sell. The complimentary color to orange is blue. Brands associated with this color include <u>Nickelodeon</u> and the <u>Home Depot</u>.

Yellow – The color of the sun is associated with laughter and happiness. It is said to make people feel optimistic and youthful. In its brightest form, this color is often used to grab consumers' attention. Its complimentary color is purple. Many brands are associated with this color, including <u>Best Buy</u>, <u>McDonalds</u> and <u>Sprint</u>.

Green – Who doesn't love the color of money? This color is associated with growth, nature, wealth and can also be calming, depending on its shade. Its complimentary color is red. Brands that are associated with this color include <u>Starbucks</u> and <u>Android</u>.

Blue – This is probably the most popular color in the world, perhaps because it is the color of the sky and the sea. It is calming, and can be associated with dependability and security. It is used by many brands, especially banks. Its complimentary color is orange. Brand's associated with blue include <u>Facebook</u>, <u>Chase</u> and, of course, <u>Website Magazine</u>.

Purple – This color is associated with royalty, and therefore represents sophistication and prosperity. It is often used with anti-aging and beauty products, and can be used to soothe or calm consumers. Its complimentary color is yellow. Brands associated with this color include Taco Bell and Yahoo.

Pink – This feminine color is best associated with romance. However, depending on the shade it can also be seen as sentimental or youthful. Many times this color targets women and young girls. This color is associated with Victoria Secret's Pink line and Barbie.

Black – This is a powerful color (or absence of color). It represents authority, stability and strength, and is often seen used for expensive products. It is usually used in combination with other colors, especially white. Brands associated with this color include Nike, Adidas and Smashbox Cosmetics.

White – Simple and purity are two words that describe this color. It is often seen used in conjunction with black, or with health related products. While most brands won't only use white, many use white in at least some aspect of their color scheme, including Apple, Volkswagen and Tylenol.

Source: Allison Howen; January 19, 2012; http://www.websitemagazine.com/content/blogs/posts/archive/2012/01/19/the-meaning-behind-color.aspx

"Color is one of the most fascinating things in the world. It attracts attention, evokes emotion and can trigger the memory."

Allison Howen, WebSiteMagazine.com | January 2012

CHAPTER 5

Million Dollar Question.

'Will this work?'

Absolutely! If you have a carefully thought out plan and you know where every dollar and marketing message is going – on purpose, marketing will work for your medical practice. It's fundamental business planning 101. I've advised countless physicians across the country over the years and spoken with many at conferences and seminars who always seem always tell me the same thing, 'Traditional advertising mediums just don't get it done and I don't have the money to spend on marketing.' My response is usually, where are you spending your money? They reply, 'I don't know. I did a postcard and pay-per-click on Google for a couple of months. Neither worked very well.'

Marketing is becoming more complex and mature, wouldn't you agree? A close friend and marketing colleague of mine recently told me at lunch the other day 'the goal of any marketing program, whether online or thru print for ANY business [medical or otherwise], is to create [visual and virtual] sign-posts in the places where your customers (i.e. prospective patients) travel on the road of life. Our job as marketing agents and ad agency representatives is to create "Pattern Interrupts." Then, if we've done our job correctly, we direct that traffic to the business for more information.'

I couldn't agree more.

There's also no end to the media's coverage of the doctor shortage arising across the U.S. A few years ago it was just as dramatic and doomsday-ish as it is today. This book however, is not about policy, theory or offering ethereal solutions to an existing and growing problem in healthcare. It's about understanding your role in learning what basic tasks it takes to find and acquire new patients; you're your message(s) and marketing strategy for better and better results and how to accelerate the mastery of your marketing plan so you can continue to stay in business and hopefully one day, sell your medical practice for a lofty profit and retire with savvy business acumen and a sense of accomplishment.

The $100,000 Decision.

Growing a medical practice takes money, maybe not that much … but typically, successful [primary care, specialty and family] medical practices across the U.S. that we've seen and worked with budget between 3% to 8% of their annual budget. But to the un-learned medical professionals, when we think about marketing, we think it's going to cost a lot of money to find out what's going to stick to the wall and actually work.

The best way to overcome this unrest in your mind and wallet is to create a written plan. Tell your dollars where they are going to be spent on paper, on purpose. Wouldn't you feel more comfortable knowing exactly where every dollar is going before you spent them? Sure you would.

The average family out-of-pocket expenditures in 2013 now exceed $20,000 per year. The growth of retail medicine, direct primary care, urgent care, concierge medicine and nurse-staffed wellness clinics are increasing provider choice – allowing patients more affordable and faster options for a patient. By late 2014, 80 million lives will be buying their own health insurance, thereby increasing health plan choices for millions of prospective patients.

Proper, well-thought out, methodical and planned marketing plans show you where you will spend your money. It's up to you to decide where you will actually spend these dollars. That in itself takes some time and research.

Impulsive May Mean Broke

Since marketing budgets for small and medium medical practices are generally small, you cannot afford to over-spend, nor under-spend. You can't afford to be impulsive either. In working with hundreds of small businesses over the years, we have found that the majority have wasted at least 70% of their marketing and advertising budgets because they really never learned, edited and mastered their marketing activities. They simply used the trial and error method and at times, focused on the urgent task when a supposedly 'great deal' came their way. This can torpedo any budget and waste a lot of money – don't market your medical practice because you saw a competitor do something or a 'great deal' came your way.

Today, I've learned that in order to be successful in navigating a marketing map/plan, you must pay to play. Sponsoring a local middle-school soccer team and putting your name on the jerseys doesn't come free. Participating in local health fair usually is accompanied by an entry fee. Mailing postcards to your patients encouraging them to see your new office location isn't free. Knowing you must allow 3% to 8% of your annual budget each year for specific marketing tasks before we begin down the path of learning can be a difficult pill to swallow. But remember, there are no shortcuts. Very rarely will new patients find you by accident. Steven Covey said "Most of us spend too much time on what is urgent and not enough time on what is important."

Key Performance Indicators.

Key Performance Indicators (KPI), also known as Key Success Indicators (KSI), help all medical practice's define and measure progress toward organizational goals (Source: About.com). Once a private practice has analyzed its mission, identified all its audience, and defined its goals, it needs a way to measure progress toward those goals. Key Performance/Success Indicators are those measurements.

Many aspects of your medical practice are measurable. In selecting your KPIs, limiting them to topics that are essential to reaching your quarterly and annual goals is very important. Keeping the number of KPIs you follow modest enough to keep your staff's attention focused on achieving those same KPIs is also crucial. Let's take a look at a few here.

Patient Indicators

There are a variety of ways to measure patient satisfaction. Verbal questions with later documented notes, patient feedback forms, social media surveys, social media comments and recommendations recorded on your Practice Facebook or Google+ Business Page -- and other such methods are great ways to quantify and examine patient satisfaction. We might think that after a month or two of operating in the new year that everything is going smoothly, but there are usually small things that patients pick up on and can suggest that you (or in many cases, your staff) could do better. Documenting and examining these KPIs quarterly or even annually at the very least will help you make small, and sometimes critical, improvements.

The most successful medical practices are the ones that communicate regularly with the majority (if not all) of their patients on a routine basis that makes their customer (I.e. patient) feel like the doctor is reaching out and maintaining a connection. It doesn't have to be face-to-face either. Many times, a simple text, Skype visit or phone call will suffice. However, if your front-office employees are not specifically asking each patient whether they've visited your practice in the past and **'is there anything else we can do to improve your next visit?'** ... this KPI can be difficult to track and start to increase annual patient attrition.

One example we can all relate to is a recent trip to the grocery store. We've all heard a check-out counter employee ask us 'did you find everything you were looking for today?' While this type of service may seem inconsequential, it still means something in the service industry. Think about what questions you'd like to be asked and ask your employees to do the same. You'll probably be surprised at the responses.

Staff Indicators

Did you realize that a significant number of patients leave their primary care provider each year because of ill-tempered or rude personnel employed by the doctor's office? The same is true in other healthcare specialties such as: chiropractic care; dental; pediatric; dermatology; etc. That's right. Often the staff member has been employed for several years and the doctor believes they are indispensable.

The following staff performance indicators will help you keep track of data so you can monitor how well your employees are impacting the success of your practice. Pay attention to the total labor cost indicator, especially if you're a relatively new concierge-style medical practice owner (less than 5 years), because it centers on how your staff impacts your renewals and patient volume.

Total Labor Cost

Total labor cost is one of the largest expenses you'll incur as a medical office owner. In a lot of medical practice office settings, approximately 38% of the practices' annual expenditures are paid to employees and part-time staff. Hence, the reason you must consistently keep track of this. According to an article in the *Houston Chronicle,* labor cost should range on average from 25 to 35 percent of your total expenses. Total labor cost includes salary or hourly wages, benefits, insurance, retirement, and bonuses that you pay to yourself and your employees. (Source: SmallBusiness.chron.com)

Labor Hours

How many hours do your employees work during a certain time frame? You should compare these hours against your sales to measure the productivity of your staff.

Turnover

Count the positions you employ, and then divide this number by the number of people you've employed during a certain period of time. For example, if you have two staff positions and you've employed six people in the last year; your staff turnover is 1/3 or 30 percent.

Patient Attrition

How many patients DO NOT come back after the first visit to your practice each year? Survey these patients to determine their reasons. If is often advisable to have an outside or objective party conduct the survey as a patient may be reticent to reveal dissatisfaction with the staff or doctor's service directly to a staff member or to the doctor directly.

"You have to also appreciate the lost art of customer service so long ago forgotten when visiting a healthcare institution. Many times my clients (notice I do not use the word "patients") have noted why they refer their friends to my practice. It is the attention to detail, always delivering exactly what is promised and then some, and keeping their unique needs positioned first with a flexibility to offer new programs or meet needs as quickly as they are identified. This is the cornerstone of customer service."

Dr. C.B. | Family Medicine | Arizona

Staff Interactions At Your Medical Practice That Should <u>Never</u> Happen

The lobby of your medical practice and reception area tells more to your patients than anywhere else in your practice. If it's furnished well, tidy and the staff working in this area is well-trained, helpful, smiling and friendly, this can be a good thing. But on the other hand, it can also be a very bad thing.

Each day, you want patients to walk-into your practice, not judge it. So, make sure you do the following things:

Make patients feel welcome. Every patient at your practice should feel welcome. That means greeting each patient as they arrive with a smile (even if your staff doesn't feel like it) and being friendly and go out of your way to be courteous at all times. If you have a service window in your lobby area, remember that your staff represents you and the demeanor of your practice, so they have to be smiling and friendly at all times.

Don't be too casual. The flip side of not being friendly enough is being a bit too friendly. Your service window staff should never interrupt a conversation. And no matter how casual the atmosphere around your practice is, your staff must always be professional. Even if someone is in pain, aggravated or disruptive, they deserve to be treated with kindness and respect.

Don't hide things. Nothing is worse than finding out you owe money from a previous visit, you owe more than a co-pay (if applicable in your practice), or your doctor is on vacation and you'll be seeing his colleague. According to ConciergeMedicineToday.com, these are the most common complaints among patients inside a primary care and family medicine office. Service window staff shouldn't lie to patients, deceive them, or be anything other than honest. Is there a delay? Tell the patients as soon as possible. Is there an upcharge for a certain test that was performed? Make sure to mention it. And always let patients know of any increase in pricing of your services and whether the practice is going to be closed on certain upcoming holidays before they leave.

Do not argue with patients. This might seem obvious, but it's important. The phrase, *"The customer is always right"* is a cliché for a reason! When a patient complains, employees should do their best to listen and help. Try to diffuse the situation by understanding and validating their feelings. You should try to fix a problem when possible, or refer the patient to the doctor or office manager if there's nothing certain staff can do. Never, ever fight with patients or dispute their complaints, even if they're wrong. If it's something they are arguing with you about in the lobby, take the conversation to another part of the practice to discuss it. Nothing makes your practice look worse than bad word of mouth, arguing or gossip in front of current patients.

Don't make the patient feel rushed. This is concierge medicine. There shouldn't be a rush! Did you know that one third of patients leave a medical practice because they were over-promised and underserved? That's right. According to *The Direct Primary Care Journal,* if you promise no-wait appointments, no rushed visits, deliver on your promises. When patients come to your practice, it's for relief and peace of mind. What they don't want is to feel rushed and pushed out of the office so the next patient can be served. Isn't that why you got into this practice in the first place? No matter how crazy the office gets or how many people are waiting on a busy day, make sure patients feel as relaxed and comfortable as possible.

Ask if the patient for their advice. This is a simple action that can really make you and your employees look like you care about the service you provide … and you do, right? The patient has an opinion if you will simply ask them … 'did we take care of all your needs today?' Asking your patients for their opinion and they will share it with you. It could be the best question you ever asked and result in a patient referral or another year or month of membership from someone who was thinking about cancelling their membership with your medical practice until you simply listened to them that day.

The most important thing for a medical practice to remember is to always be friendly, courteous, helpful, and professional. By keeping these tips in mind, you and your staff can avoid big blunders and keep you from losing patients.

"Unfortunately, most of us have little sense of our talents and strengths, much less the ability to build our lives around them. Instead, guided by our parents, by our teachers, by our managers, and by psychology's fascination with pathology, we become experts in our weaknesses and spend our lives trying to repair these flaws, while our strengths lay dormant and neglected."

Firing A Rock Star.

I can't tell you how many times I've spoken to a doctor's office that shares with me the same story ... 'I had an employee who didn't believe in my medical practice model and they were telling patients to go somewhere else. I should have done something but they've been with me for years.'

Did you know that one of the top ten reasons why patients leave their physician is because they don't like your staff? That's right and while passionate employees produce better results – keeping someone who has been loyal to you for years but you know deep down isn't good for business can cause more harm than good to your bottom line. The best way to spark passion in your front office employees, nurses and other staff is to demonstrate your own passion — but don't be a cheerleader at staff meetings. Here are three simple ways to authentically show your enthusiasm and inspire others:

Have everyone share a success story once a month at your staff meeting. This will help build camaraderie among your staff as well as lasting memories that help foster the kind of stories that you and your staff want to achieve from month-to-month.

Focus on the positive. Author and business consultant Marcus Buckingham wrote a book about this. He writes ... *Unfortunately, most of us have little sense of our talents and strengths, much less the ability to build* *our lives around them. Instead, guided by our parents, by our teachers, by our managers, and by psychology's fascination with pathology, we become experts in our weaknesses and spend our lives trying to repair these flaws, while our strengths lie dormant and neglected.*

Too often we focus on the bad thing(s) that went wrong. While this is necessary to discuss at times in our business, we need to learn as managers of businesses to encourage and help employees grow and use their strengths at work. Employees know when a doctor truly cares about his or her practice. Passionate doctors can't help but talk about what's working well and try to find ways to fix what isn't. So, help your employees nurture their strengths month-to-month — you'll be glad you did!

Set goals and expectations. One of the reasons that mega-churches are growing so fast across the U.S. is that they have set expectations with their audience week in and week out. It's no different in a doctor's office. You should know exactly what to expect when you walk in and if you're going to be greeted with a smile, an ill-tempered staff member that needs to find another job or you'll be given a bill. Which scenario sounds best to you?

This doesn't mean unattainable workloads. Passionate docpreneurs should inspire and challenge their employees and patients to do their best, without overloading them. A great tip is to break your goals and expectations into little tiny goals creating easy wins for your team and your patients. This constant state of winning will be a guaranteed formula for success. Everyone wants to be with the winning team. Success breeds success and it is infectious.

Encourage everyone on your staff to be part of the relational, healthy lifestyle process. I believe that in order for sustained, healthy lifestyle change to occur, we have to grow together with those we surround ourselves with. This happens best inside a doctor's office when together, patients, employees and the doctor(s) are prioritizing intentional relationships and we're all seeking the same goal. Walked out, this means that if a patient is struggling with a weight problem, broken their arm or coping with a more serious chronic condition, they want to know that it's not just the doctor who cares — but the receptionist on my way out who asks me if I'm okay too.

"Keep your staff happy.
Staff plays a key role in keeping patients happy.
Make sure front office and nursing staff develops a
strong relationship with your patients."

Dr. E | Internal Medicine Physician | Buckhead, GA

Takeaway

As your practice grows, your human resources can become more formalized. According to Entrepreneur.com, check-ins with new staff should happen at multiple intervals, after the first and second weeks as well as after the first 30, 60 and 90 days to ensure they have the tools they need and can get questions answered.

Hopefully, with the use of your office manager now dedicated to helping you in the new hire process, you should maybe spend less than two hours a week on talent acquisition and hiring.

"I want an entrepreneurial culture," says one physician from New York City. "Hiring is part of growing and we need to make sure our type of practice does it right. We have a lot to live up to as doctors. Let's get our employees attitude and service capabilities right."

A large, rapidly growing medical practice must evolve its hiring practices and empower staff to take the reins.

"We asked hundreds of medical doctors 'what is your largest annual expense?' Our responses from 2009 to present tell us that most doctors' offices spend about 38% of their annual income on Staff/employees followed closely by Leased Office Space/Mortgage at 24%. In a close third, Malpractice Insurance at 19% and equipment at 5% and rising.

Source: Direct Primary Care Journal, © 2013

Marketing And Advertising Indicators

This list of indicators is more important to medical practice business owners who actually spend money on marketing. And a large majority of doctors do. Most doctors spend as little as 1%-2% on marketing and advertising each year where some doctors choose to spend more – surveys tell us as much as 14% of their annual income. Many new medical practice owners start up without putting any funding into this area, and thus don't need to track this data.

While it can be very difficult to grow a private practice in a difficult economy, most medical doctors are thriving ... increasing their annual revenue each year in the first five years from $100K per year to $400,000 or more per year.

Since 2009, *Concierge Medicine Today*, a news and industry-wide resource agency for the concierge medicine and direct-pay medical field has been asking doctors in these offices two important questions. First, 'how long does it take to recruit or persuade a new patient to become a patient in your practice?' Second, 'what form of marketing is most productive when trying to attract new patients to your practice?' The answers to these questions are very important. (Source: AskTheCollective.org, 2009-2013)

How long does it take to recruit or persuade 'one' new patient to become a patient in your practice?

- 49% - Four or more months
- 23% - Three to four months
- 4% - One to two months
- 13% - Two to four weeks
- 11% - One to two weeks

What form of marketing is most productive when trying to attract new patients to your practice?
- 16% - Hire a Marketing/PR Firm
- 14% - Letter with Brochure
- 13% - Word of Mouth Referral

So, with a natural attrition rate of roughly 10% (Source: ConciergeMedicineToday.com, 2011-2013), is only one of the following ways listed above enough to sustain a practice year after year? A doctor will know when they consistently track and measure the following KPIs in this category:

- Marketing and public relations (PR) costs
- Response rates
- Sales inquiry conversion rate
- Press mentions

Sales And Service Indicators

These indicators center on your bottom line. Your sales and service costs will determine whether your concierge medical practice is succeeding financially.

Service cost percentage: How much do you spend per to make sure your practice is 'servicing' your patient to the level they'd like? This may include equipment expenditures, magazine subscriptions, beverage delivery, television/cable costs, vitamins, recipe cards, etc. Think of these as the non-medical and non-health related add-ons that patients know make your practice different from other doctor's offices in the area. These services are not part of your square footage fee in your lease agreement or mortgage.

You usually calculate these costs as a percentage of your total business expense. You measure it by adding your purchases for the week and comparing those figures to your weekly sales. Depending on the type of services you serve and provide to your patients, this number can range from 5 to 15 percent. (***Note:*** Doctors' offices that choose the route of operating a franchised practice model will have a lower service cost potentially due to the buying power, cost control systems the franchisor can bring or limitation of services they accept inside a new franchised practice.)

Weekly Sales. This number is one of the standard sales-related numbers that every doctor's office looks at. As you may expect, weekly sales can vary widely from one practice to the next. The key number to look at is any change you find from week to week and how it compares to previous years.

Sales Per Head. One of the most used performance indicators is sales per head, which you calculate by dividing your total sales by the number of patients you serve. To do this, you must make sure your point-of-sale system or your employees and staff are properly accounting for the number of patients each sale covers.

You can calculate your sales per head at different times or shifts throughout the day, week, month or quarter. For a more detailed understanding of this metric, you can track your sales per head each week or month to look for reasons for positive or negative trends. For example, your sales per head may trend downward when you run discounted product-related (i.e. add-on) specials.

Best (and worst) Selling Items. Check the weekly sales from your receipts or point-of-sale system to help you determine which services from your menu items are either consistently selling out or simply taking up space on your menu board.

NOTE: For more business tips, articles related to the concierge medical marketplace and trends, visit our TRENDS Blog at www.ConciergeMedicineToday.com.

10 Not-So-Obvious Direct Mail Mistakes.

There are the obvious direct mail mistakes like no offer or call to action, the wrong phone number or web address, or misspelled words. Most marketers don't need to read an article to figure those out. This article focuses on lesser-known mistakes that can make the difference between success and failure. (Source: Source: Directmailtools.com | APRIL 2012) **Here are 10:**

1) **Cheap Offers.** There is a tendency for marketers and business owners to worry about "giving away the house." Offers like "10% off your next purchase" or "Free Shipping with you next order of $100 or more" are ok if you're targeting current customers that need a small nudge to make an incremental purchase. But if you're going after new customers, "Free" is always the most powerful word in direct mail. A new customer may cost you $200 or more (do the math!), so giving away something free at a cost to you of $50 or so, may be a no-brainer.

2) **Short Copy.** There is yet another tendency for marketers to think "we need to keep it short and sweet." They use clean graphics with few words. The thought is that interested prospects will call or go to the website. In direct mail, long copy (more words) usually outperforms short copy. Write as much as you need to fully explain your product and its functions/benefits. Don't assume too much knowledge on the part of your prospect. Finally, get someone's opinion that's not an industry "insider."

3) **Small Card.** Small cards (regular postcards) are useful. They're cheap and mail First Class for the same cost as Standard Class. If your product is simple, like a local coffee shop, or if you're mailing to

current customers that already know your brand and product, small cards are great. If your product is more complicated or relies heavily on branding (like photos of past work, or product photos), use a larger card. Larger cards get noticed more and can be chock-full of information.

4) **No Frequency.** It's rare that your mailing coincides with a prospect's need to buy. Especially if you're doing business-to-business sales. In most cases, you're mailing simply places a "seed" of awareness so that when your prospect does need your product or service, they think of you. Those "seeds" need to be planted continuously or the awareness dies.   There's also research that shows that the more a person is exposed to your brand, the more that person has a "favorable" impression of your brand.

5) **Bad Timing.** It's very obvious that you don't market snowmobiles in July. But on the other hand, we see home improvement businesses like landscapers marketing their product late in the summer and avoiding the prime marketing season in the spring. The rational is that, "I'm busy in the spring and I need business for late in the summer." The better strategy is to market when prospects are buying. If you don't have the capacity to do the work, offer an incentive to put the work off until you do have the capacity.

6) **Small Mailing Quantities.** Direct Mail, like just about all advertising Medias, relies on small percentages of respondents. You mail out 100 cards and hope to have one call. On the other hand, if you're testing a direct mail piece and expect the one call on

mailing 100 cards to be your proof of success, you are sadly mistaken. The reality is that you may not get that call. Then, do you know if the mailing is a failure? Not really. You haven't mailed enough cards to statistically be confident that the results are correct. To be statistically confident, you will need to mail anywhere from 3,000 (acceptable confidence) to 10,000 (higher confidence).

7) **The Wrong Offer.** Some offers are easy: "Bring this coupon in and get a free cup of coffee." But others get to be more complicated. It's difficult to sell certain software's, products or services by simply saying, "This is what it does," and "you get $100 off." The more costly the service or product, the more a prospect wants lots of information. They need samples, or trials, or white papers, or webinars, or booklets. Instead of asking for the sale, offer free information to simply get the lead.

8) **Standard Class Postage with Time-Sensitive Mailings.** Standard Class can save you a substantial amount on your mailings. But if the "sale" announcement comes 2 days after your sale ends, the savings are moot. Standard Class takes on average 7 to 10 days for delivery, but you can't even count on that. You cards will get delivered, but just never count on timing.

9) **Standard Class Postage with Business Addresses.**
We've just had bad experiences with using Standard Class to mail cards to businesses. The feedback we get is, "many of my customers didn't receive the mailing." If the address and contact information isn't exact, they might not get delivered. Also, Standard Class mailings sometimes tend to get tossed out by mailroom clerks or other "gatekeepers." The great thing about First Class is that if the mailing doesn't get delivered, it gets returned to you.

10) **No Contact Information.** Ok, this is obvious. No phone number, no address, no directions, no web address, no e-mail address, etc. It happens all the time.

Secrets From Experts In Direct Mail Marketing.

Source: Directmailtools.com | APRIL 2012

Q: Is sending someone an article/tear sheet with a hand-written note still a good idea?

Answer: Yes! Anything handwritten is 300 times more likely to be opened and read by the recipient. Be sure the white envelope you use also has the address in your own handwriting too!

Q: What's the most affordable form of direct mail with the highest return on investment?

Answer: Postcards

Q: Where are affordable places to invest advertising

dollars in my local community?

Answer: Local magazines and HOA Newsletters and Help Wanted Advertising Sections in local area publications.

Should I Send A Letter To Your Colleagues In Healthcare, If So, About What And Why?

Q: Would sending a letter to some of my colleagues, maybe outside my specialty, which is located in my area, help me acquire new patients?

Answer: Yes! Physicians at a recent conference I attended in November 2013 talked about this topic a lot. It does work. The first thing you want to do is collect a list of the practitioners in your area names and addresses. Address the letter to them personally (i.e. the doctor), thank them for reading your letter (this might sound weird … but it works, so be sure to include it). Try to solve their problems. What value and services would their patients have by coming to see you?

Last, state near the end of the letter that 'you eagerly anticipate collaborating with them in the very near future. You might even want to ask them questions also. For example, what type of patients do you treat or would like for your practice to refer to them? Are they comfortable handling Medicare patients? etc.

"Working as a hospitalist in a local hospital makes a significant difference with regard to referrals."

Dr. E | Internal Medicine Physician | Buckhead, GA

CHAPTER 6

quote 1

Return On Effort.

This is probably the most important chapter in the entire book. This chapter was the hardest one to put into words because no to my knowledge has ever truly focused on those activities inside a medical practice that go unnoticed but are so important to do each and every week to grow a practice and acquire more patients.

I love this quote by John Maxwell that says "If you start today to do the right thing, you are already a success even if it doesn't show yet." This statement encompasses what it means to work hard, exert an endless amount of energy and hours into your business.

The same holds true today in your practice. There are so many things you can do to help your business grow.

Single-Serve Coffee Brew Stations Making Big Impression With Patients

Occasionally you might run out of the house without your hot cup of tea or favorite blend of coffee at your side. If you're like me, you love the convenience of a fresh, cup of tea or coffee when you're running late.

The Keurig K-Cup coffee makers and other single-serve and pod coffee/tea brewers have come into businesses with a flurry of excitement over the past two years. Patients spending any amount of time in your office will appreciate the convenience and employees of concierge medical practices love the easy, no mess — clean-up they provide.

In recent months, these single coffee cup brewers have become much more affordable and stylish. Some of the larger big-box wholesale clubs even sell such devices to their members with 60 or more K-Cups included with the price of the coffee maker. So, if you have the traditional-style coffee maker which involves making a full pot of coffee, you're behind the trend...!

"One-third of Walgreens Vaccinations Are Administered During Off-Clinic Hours, Implications for Improving Vaccination Access and Convenience."

Study conducted in collaboration with the University of Southern California School of Pharmacy and published in the September/October issue of Annals of Family Medicine; Deerfield, IL., September 11, 2013

Earlier Hours Inside "Modern" Medical Practices Becoming The Norm

If your mornings are anything like mine, you prefer to schedule the majority of your health exams and check-ups right away. In fact, the earlier the better! I'll take the first possible appointment or even the second visit of the day because I know that I that my physician(s) are revving up for a busy day — and they and I, need to get our day moving.

I'm a big fan of practices which cater to the patient with hours starting at 6:30am or even 7am. Just last week, I visited a few into a dental practice in North Atlanta, GA area and was pleasantly surprised at the early morning or after 6pm appointments they've made available to their patients every Monday, Tuesday and Thursday.

MARKETING TIP #116

*"You should use a site that has a Google PageRank of 4
and above because sites with no PageRank
will lower the credibility of the PR.*

Sending Press Releases

Sending out press releases is a great way to get picked up by news sites and blogs. If you choose sites that link back to you, you can increase your ranking on Google. But which press release sites should you use?

Press releases are becoming a successful way of Internet advertising. These not only provide valuable inbound links, but also increase your reputation, brand, and expertise and web traffic ... thus your chances of getting located by search engines and contacted by local media for interviews. But, all your efforts will get waste if the press release is not newsworthy or if it is distributed via a non-credible PR distribution site.

There are only a few PR services providers who can provide you maximum visibility and credibility on the Internet. Follow these guidelines while choosing a press release distribution site:

You should use a site that has a Google PageRank of 4 and above because sites with no PageRank will lower the credibility of the PR.

Approach a site that allows you to optimize the press release for search engines by using header tags, tagging, anchor text and other SEO techniques.

Keep away from sites that use No Follow tags. These tags are inserted into website code in order to stop the search engine from finding the site.

So, here are a few press release sites that provide both free and paid distribution services. The list will help you in finding a reliable PR distribution service provider who will get you maximum visibility on the World Wide Web.

Free-Press-Release.com – PageRank 5- The best part of using it is that you can place banners on the press release that will point to your website. The paid service offered by this website has better ranking and many SEO benefits.

Free-Press-Box.com – PageRank 5- Submitting your press release on to this site is really easy. It accepts free submissions as well as paid submissions.

Free-Press-Index.com – PageRank 4- This PR site allows for instant submissions for free with inbound links to your site in place. For the paid service, they charge close $60, and distribute the release among 250,000 subscribers and journalists.

NewswireToday.com - PageRank 6- The design of website is not good and you will difficulty in navigation also. It offers common free distribution tools and the premium service will enable you to give logo, product picture and insert other features in the press release.

1888PressRelease.com - PageRank 5- The site has good page rank and also gets good traffic. Active links are allowed. If you opt for their paid service, the placement will be better and you will get features like image galleries & permanent archiving.

I-Newswire.com - PageRank 6- You get free PR distribution option to sites and search engines. If you opt for premium membership, the only difference is that you can add graphics on the PR.

SB Wire.com - PageRank 4- It is specially dedicated site too small to medium-sized businesses. With the free service you can submit your press release and get connected to bloggers in your niche. For the paid program, they offer many packages starting from $14.95 to $99.95 (for unlimited search engine friendly releases).

Free-Press-Release-Center.info - PageRank 4- It is a clean looking site and the increasing traffic level will increase the PageRank soon. You can do PR submission and distribution; include one link with the anchor text while availing free service. The paid service enables you to give three links, permanent archiving and has many more features.

Online-PR-News.com - PageRank 5- The free submission service allows you to give one live link in the contact information area, you can have a search engine friendly title and Meta. These releases will be archived. The paid submissions include social sharing buttons, and you can place 3 anchor text links, and also spice up your release with a suitable image.

Add-PR.com - PageRank 3- This is a site, that allows only free PR submissions. You can leave a live link in the contact details section. The site is clean and crisp, and allows the exposure to potentially thousands of Internet media outlets.

Big-News.biz – PageRank 4- This free submission site allows for easy registration, and you can quickly start on submitting your release. It allows for a link in the contact details section.

News-By-Company.com - PageRank 3- This is free press release site, for small and medium business enterprises. It allows for a link in the anchor text and one in the contact information section. The interface is clean and the site has good credibility.

PRLog.org - PageRank 6- It is an ordinary and functional looking site but results are good. It gives free distribution service for Google News and other search engines. Inbound links are allowed and the site is also properly optimized for search engines. You can schedule the press release.

Wide-PR.com - PageRank 4- This free PR site is pretty good with its services, as with every free submission, you get live links automatically integrated into your free press release. You can also load 3 images and also your company logo. Needless to say you can use optimized tags and keywords.

Press-Release-Point.com - PageRank 5- This is a free site where you can sign up for either distribution of the release or for writing releases or both. It allows for 4 links in the body and 3 links in the contact section.

OpenPR.com - PageRank 5-This service distribution site is based in Germany. It provides free submission and distribution along with SEO benefits.

PRLeap.com - PageRank 5-The site is said to deliver reasonable results. It is nice and clean. The price of press release starts from $49 – $149, depending on the level of service you have opted for. The distribution is done on search engines, RSS feeds and newswires. .

Press-Media-Wire.com - PageRank 4- This paid submission site offers three packages ranging from $19 to $99 per release. They assure you visibility with tools like video and pictures.

PR-Fire.co.uk - PageRank 5- This paid site offers tailor made packages from £299, where they do all the work from sourcing a story to the final copy. They also allow for a free submission onto their site.

PR.com - PageRank 6- The domain name is superb but you can say the services are not so appealing. The site has one free basic service and two paid services of $199 and $499. You can give full company profile by taking paid option.

"The investment you will make into community events isn't always monetary and simply costs you the time of someone employed by your practice, often the doctors themselves. The reward of this work is amazing – so get started today!"

Community Events.

Activities that are more often overlooked for two reasons are the use of community events to enhance the image of your practice and create top of mind awareness (TOMA). The first reason that community events are overlooked is because doctors don't know how or where to begin. The second is, it takes time. Usually, someone in the practice, often the Office Manager, to spend a few hours each month on the phone making connections with local businesses, churches, rotary and other such clubs in the area, attending business networking social meetings, etc.

The investment you will make into community events isn't always monetary and simply costs you the time of someone employed by your practice, often the doctors themselves. It's actually best, if the doctors attend the majority of these meetings to create a face to go with the name and brand of the practice.

Create Your Own.

Another way community events are facilitated and become a real, operating marketing activity in your practice that drives patients into your practice by positive word of mouth is to Create Your Own Event(s) each quarter. This might be a partnership with a charity during the holidays or declare a month "Fiber Awareness

Month," etc. This is where you can be creative and encourage your staff to participate.

Church Sponsored Efforts

If one of your staff attends a local church in the area around your practice, and they probably do, put your creative hat on and think of ways your medical practice can help serve the local church. One way might be contacting the Office Administrator at the church or Pastor and talking to them about sponsoring a health fair on an upcoming Saturday afternoon.

Another idea could be free flu shots for all church staff. Your staff and the church staff probably can quickly and easily create multiple events in which your practice could help serve. It doesn't cost you much money and you're doing a tremendous service to the community. Plus, you're creating great word of mouth PR in the local area. Now, every single one of those church members are prospective patients. Imagine that!

Sponsor Local Sports Team

Local middle school athletic soccer games and high school games are well attended by Moms, Dads, Aunts, Uncles and Grandparents. This is probably your core target audience. Place a phone call and send a letter to your local middle school and high school athletic department or even private school sports programs and ask them if you could sponsor a team. More often than not, putting your name on the soccer jerseys of some 2nd graders will cost your practice less than $500 for the entire season.

Each time that team takes the field your name is on the front or the back of those team jerseys. You might even be able to hang a vinyl banner near the fence. Pick one, two or even three sports and keep your medical practice top of mind among parents, children, students and teachers throughout the year among different sports.

Hospice: Sr. Centers; Living Facilities

Local senior center office administrators and admitting staff are always looking for quality primary care physicians, dental care clinics and other healthcare practitioners to refer to. Many times, loved ones are completing paperwork in an area unfamiliar to the senior care center and don't know who the quality healthcare providers in that area are. Visit the senior care centers and assisted living centers in your area.

Talk directly to the staff and tell them about what you do, where you're located, ask to leave a few brochures, fliers and business cards to pass out to visitors. Don't let this be a one-time visit though. Stop by each month and try to talk to the same staff you previously met. Follow-up with them monthly and ask how things are going and how you, your staff and medical practice can help them as well. You'll be surprised at the results a little time and a few dollars of gas cost you.

Patient Appreciation Events

We don't often think of hosting events for patients, but without them, you wouldn't have a business. Show them your appreciation throughout the year. Host an educational event and invite some or all of your most beloved patients. Talk to your staff about ways in which you can 'give back' to your patients. Maybe it's in the form of a coupon. Maybe it's a gift card. Be creative but host the event at your practice.

Speaking (Educational)

You've got so much to share with the local community but if you're not out there talking, no one is going to learn about what you have to say. Sending out letters to local Rotary Clubs, Chamber of Commerce Groups, Business Networking Events, Local Area Businesses, etc., is an important component of fostering good PR and top of mind awareness in your community.

Consider sending a letter about the various topics you'd like to speak to busy office workers about and follow up with a visit to the business and ask them if they received your letter. There are a number of health related topics that employers and businesses in your area would like to host for their employees. Be the conduit that can educate, connect and guide people back to your practice because of your expertise.

Corporate Health Fairs

A lot of companies, colleges and hospitals host health fairs. Many of which, know there are a lot of health care providers in the area but they don't actually know who they are. These health fairs typically have an entry fee of less than $300 dollars. Participating in local health fairs and getting to know your colleagues, neighbors and businesses in the area is a great way of networking and getting your name out there in places you've never been.

Do you work in an office park? When was the last time you went door to door and introduced you to other businesses? I bet you probably have been leasing that space for years now and don't even know your neighbors around you or across the street.

Take an hour out of your week and some business cards, a flier or a practice brochure and go shake some hands and hug some necks. You'll be glad you started the process of networking.

Chamber Events

Chamber of Commerce event Staff are always looking for local area businesses to come in and talk about specific topics. This is one of the easiest and most cost effective ways to get your face known among business leaders, your target audience and the community. Contact the local Chamber and ask them about what events are coming up in the next month and how you could help.

Support Group Hosting

You're in the business of helping people, right? Well, maybe around the corner and down the street there is a diabetes support group that needs a place to meet on Saturday mornings or Wednesday evenings for an hour. Consider announcing to your patients that your practice is hosting weekly or monthly activities to support any number of the following health topics: diabetes; cancer; over-eating; nutrition; weight loss; etc.

Now is the time and way you and your practice can really make an impact.

Cooking Creations Classes

Maybe you like to cook. Maybe your staff has a new recipe or a long-time patient has a testimonial and healthy recipe they'd like to share. Consider sending out a flier monthly to your patients letting them know that once a month here at the practice, you're offering free cooking classes.

If you are like most medical practice owners, you probably have a large community of patients who love to cook and eat healthy. That love for food coupled with a love for sharing your unique medical practice enables you to have the unique opportunity to grow and expand within your local community very quickly and in a passive sales-like way.

Determine what kind of cooking classes you will teach.

If you or one of your staff loves Italian cooking, or making on-the-go healthy shakes, start with these types of simple classes first. If you are an expert bread baker, offer classes in these techniques. Make a list of your skills, even skills that don't seem important to you at first. Maybe teaming up with your spouse, kids or staff is a good idea too. It's quite possible that once you go through the list, you will see ample opportunity to offer a variety of classes that patients and prospective patients will want to attend again and again.

Know the law

Check with your local department of health as well as your county clerk's office to find out if you'll need any type of special license to provide this type of service. Due to the fact that you are not selling the food, it is unlikely that you will need to have an inspection. It's a simple phone call and takes less than 5-minutes but it's best to know before you begin. Offering classes in your patients' or an employee's homes can also be an option.

Gather equipment and set up

Be sure that you have everything you will need to teach your class. Nothing looks worse than not having a key ingredient. If your class attendees will be cooking, be sure to have enough for everyone. You won't need five mixers, for example, but you will need to have ample mixing bowls, ramekins, measuring cups, spoons and ingredients.

Bonus Tip!

If your kitchen isn't properly equipped, see if you can offer classes through a local retail store (think Sur la table or William Sonoma). This can be great marketing for them and provides you a place to do your cooking. If you can't find a store to work with you, you may be able to rent the space from your commercial kitchen.

Develop your promotional materials

Add your class offerings to your medical practice brochure that can be handed out at your office, service window to patients or anywhere in the local community. Also include this promotional piece on your website.

Bonus Tip!

People love take-aways. And something that can easily be found when they put your recipe on their shelf at home. Be sure to print out enough recipe cards for everyone and on a color paper that people will know it's yours. Be sure to include your practice web site and telephone number somewhere on the card and maybe the name of your practice too. If you're doing a series of classes, make all of your recipe cards similar in shape and consider lamination too. Maybe you also want to think about a small recipe box so that when people attend each of your classes, they have an entire box or place in which to go to find all of your healthy recipes!

Plan well

You might find that your first classes will go along so well you don't need a plan, but creating a syllabus and making notes for yourself will help to ensure that you hit all the points you want to make. You don't need to plan every class to the minute, but having general points you want to go over will make teaching easier and help the class go smoothly. (See the list below for tips on creating a class syllabus)

Start Small

Once you get interest in your first set of classes; you'll need to decide if these will be a series of classes or a one-time only thing–only accept a few students. This will help you get your feet wet, allow you to try new things and help you keep your nerves down if you are nervous about your new venture.

"Cooking classes are becoming a popular and fun way to engage with your patients, teach them healthy habits and invite new faces into your practice. Physicians across the country are starting to use these events as patient referral programs and seeing big return on effort!"

Concierge Medicine Today | © 2013 | September 2013 | www.ConciergeMedicineToday.com

The Following Will Help You Create A Syllabus For Your Own Cooking Class:

Whether you're a foodie, a weekend crock-pot queen or King of the BBQ, you're a still a physician. You have knowledge about the body, clean foods and digestion that you need to share and people want to learn about. Sharing your knowledge of food, handling of meats or just plain salad tips can turn into a profitable patient-procurement strategy for your practice simply by offering cooking classes or seminars to your existing patients and their friends.

Whether you conduct them at your practice, a commercial kitchen or simply have an in-home kitchen ideal for the set-up, you can offer classes and instructional teaching in a niche area of your own choosing or offer basic and advanced cooking strategies that people will want to use and desire to learn more about. So, while leading such classes is often a lot of fun, it can also be looked at as an extension of your concierge medicine or direct-pay marketing strategy.

Before you begin, we've put together a few tips for you and your staff.

Theory before Practice

When teaching people how to cook who may not be very skilled at it, have never cooked before or have very limited knowledge, it's a good idea to start at the beginning. When you first start a cooking class, your students have to know the fundamentals of cooking. These basics of cooking can include the type of pans you will be using in your class, why you use certain utensils and detailed explanations of various cooking techniques.

You will also want to teach them the rules of the kitchen, appliance safety and knife safety. Go over what your plans are before you actually let them cook.

Prepare Handouts

Every good cooking class needs handouts. It should include information and reminders of important concepts you want them to remember. It should also include the recipes you will be showing them how to make. Try to get these done before your class even starts.

Start Small

You don't want to throw your students into a practical cooking lesson by having them cook an elaborate 5 course meal. Start with small dishes with limited ingredients. As you advance from beginner dishes to more challenging ones, you can include useful cooking tricks.

Bonus Tip!

If you're wondering how many people to invite, we recommend starting small and working your class-size up from there. Your physical environment and cooking space will also limit the amount of people. Probably 6 to ten people to begin with are a good place to start.

Using And Working With Your Local Media

Don't be intimidated. Journalists, reporters, writers and editors are not looking to expose deep, dark secrets 99% of the time. The media can and should be your friend, particularly the "Hyper local" media. "Hyper local" media meaning a group of publications, niche magazines, newsletters or localized media outlets near your business that focuses primarily on the concerns of local residents.

These media outlets might simply cover one or two zip codes around your medical practice, blog only to a certain township or geographic area, etc. HOA Newsletters are another example of "hyper local" media. You can probably think of one or two "hyper local" media or publications that you read regularly … for me, I see them at the end of my driveway once a week. In my area, they distribute and report only on the activities and happenings in my county.

Local reports typically write about local businesses starting in the area, Rotary Club meetings; special parades happening; DUI's; burglaries, and much more. Believe it or not, more people read these types of publications and HOA newsletters and blogs cover to cover before throwing them in the waste bin.

Reach out to your "hyper local" media and consider the following ways in which your medical practice can communicate with them:

- Call and tell them about a new procedure you are doing in your practice;
- Write a short press release, 3-4 paragraphs long about tests; screenings or vaccines your offering to the local community this month;
- Talk to the editors – or better yet, take them to lunch and tell them you'd like to write some educational articles. What type of content are they looking for?
- Are you treating a certain "niche" population? I.e. Senior Center(s); Homeless; Mothers; Children; etc. Tell your local media about how you're helping them.
- Have you written a book or recently been published? Tell them about it.
- Do you have unique training? Write a letter to the editors and tell them about yourself and your practice and most importantly, what services you offer to the local community.
- Write a short press release, 3-4 paragraphs long about a charitable event your participating in.

When it comes to your Doctor's Office on Facebook Page ... experts say ... "You should be more concerned about REACH versus LIKES and engagement – meaning how many people did your various posts 'reach' – not how many "Liked" it or commented on a post you made."

Be Ready When The Local Media
Asks You For An Interview

Last, be ready! If you think the media won't call, you're wrong. One day very soon they will. You need to be ready. In the book The Media Training Bible, author Brad Phillips provides Eight Ways To Deliver A Better Phone Interview.

Get out of your office: Don't sit at your desk, where you can become easily distracted by incoming emails, phone calls, and office visitors. Find an empty conference room with no distractions, and tape a "Do Not Disturb—Interview in Progress" sign on the door.

Bring your notes: It's okay to have notes in front of you during phone interviews. Be careful not to "read" them to the reporter but to use them only as memory triggers. (See lesson 94 for more about the best way to prepare notes for an interview.)

Get a headset: Telephone headsets are terrific gadgets for phone interviews. They allow you to use both of your hands to gesture, which adds emphasis to your voice, and they free you from cradling a phone to your neck in case you need to jot down a few notes during your call.

Stand: When our trainees stand, they literally "think faster on their feet." They also tend to project more authority, likely because pacing helps them use their nervous energy in a more productive manner.

Smile: Smile when appropriate. The reporter (and audience, for radio interviews) can hear your warmth radiating through the phone.

Prioritize audio quality: Speaker and cell phones have inferior sound quality and can be a barrier to easy communication. Plus, reporters may conclude, "He thinks he's too important to pick up the damn phone?" It's best to use a landline with a high-quality headset.

Click, clack, and repeat: During print interviews, listen for the sound of typing on the other end—you'll hear it when you say something that intrigues the reporter. That's your cue to slow down and repeat what you've just said to make sure the reporter has time to capture every word. Also, don't hesitate to check in with the reporter by asking whether your explanation made sense.

Now, what did I just say? If you think you may have mangled a key quote, you can ask the reporter to read it back to you (some reporters will oblige, others won't). Reporters may not be willing to change something you said if you don't like the way you said it—but they usually will if you said something factually inaccurate.

Source:
http://www.mrmediatraining.com/2013/04/24/eight-ways-to-deliver-a-better-phone-interview/

MARKETING TIP # 749

Listing sites such as: Vitals.com; HealthyGrades.com; ZocDoc.com; GetListed.org; EverydayHealth.org; RateMDs.com; DrScore.com; Switchboard.com, Yahoo!, Bing, Google Local, YP.com, Kudzu.com and AngiesList.com allows searchers (i.e. prospective patients) to narrow their search by categories of services and view past patient reviews. It would make sense to take the time to monitor monthly these comments, tie your services to as many of these categories as possible so that your business appears in more instances when a person is searching. Most of these sites are free. Some require a subscription. Start using them today!

CHAPTER 7

Going Digital.

It is easy to forget how integrated social is in our lives now; everyone knows the growth of social has been huge over the last 5+ years, but what about in the last 12 months? Well, below are just a <u>few of those stats</u>, we've pulled out a few key stats that we thought are of great interest...

- 49% of Twitter users rarely login
- Facebook acquires 63.46% market share of Internet visitors each month
- 1 in 4 Americans watch a YouTube video every single day
- 53% of employees research potential job candidates on social networks
- Facebook has 310 million unique visitors every day
- Stumbleupon gets more daily traffic than Twitter

4 Secret Strategies To Creating A Massive Web Presence, Getting Found Online, Generating Traffic & Building Your List.

A mentor of mine and online marketing and article writing expert, Jeff Herring discusses the purpose of 'why' exactly businesses should be online. To summarize, he says...

#1) Get Found

Because there are millions of sites on the Internet, the first and most important step is getting found. Having a strong online presence allows you to erect "multiple sign posts" leading to your information. And here is the bottom line: Getting found is everything. In all the noise in your niche, when you get found, you are heads above everyone else.

#2) Get Viewed

The steps here are simple – once found, prospects can view your information contained in the signposts you have erected. As prospects begin to consume your information and realize that you are knowledgeable what you are talking about, they begin to know, like and trust you. You can then direct them to other resources you may have, which leads to the next step.

#3) Get Traffic

One of the beauties of having many sign posts in your Social Marketing system is that you can use these signposts to direct prospects (traffic) where you want them to go. In this way you are not chasing traffic, you are getting yourself in front of where the traffic is going and then directing it where you want it to go.

#4) Get Profits

When traffic is properly directed it turns into profits. If getting found is the most important thing in Social Marketing, then what the prospect finds once they get there is a very close second. When the prospect finds more good information from you that are helpful to them, followed by an offer of a paid resource that is going to help them even more, they are much more likely to buy from you.

We're living in unprecedented times. We are probably preaching to the choir for many of you, but here's the thing. When marketing and branding your business in social media, there is no middle-man. The playing field is leveled. Everybody has the opportunity to build their own Profile and pages and grow their own business.

If you're wondering where to get started, I'd suggest examining other marketing channels to expand your reach. The best part is, for the most part, they're free!

First, you might have created other social channels that you're not currently using for business purposes. Twitter, Google+, LinkedIn, YouTube, Friendster, and Pinterest. All of these are great social media platforms for marketing your business. You might also have another channel like your own blog subscribers or your email list.

Second, if you have a local business, a physical establishment, think about the eyeballs of your current customers. What are they reading when they are inside your business? Here's a bonus tip for you – if you have a local office that you see customers at, look at the pieces of literature and brochures you are using to promote various programs, events and your business. It never ceases to amaze me how so many businesses don't put their social channels on their business cards, brochures, eye-level on the internal door(s) as they exit, in the restroom, etc.

Simply putting a statement "Come and chat with us on Facebook" will help your users engage with your brand online. And, there's no better time to get them to like your page or say something positive about their most recent visit with you than while they are thinking about it. Place your social media channel logos and a simple phrase on your window signage, decals on windows or mirrors, walls, cash register or right on the products or forms you give to current customers.

Create A Low-Risk, Irresistible Offer, Maybe 2 Or 3.

As the Senior Director of Marketing at marketing firm and the Editor of a physician trade journal for a certain niche of the physician population, the biggest, singular mistake I see doctors make is...they don't have an irresistible low-risk offer for a prospective patient that entices them to want to take the next step and learn more about their business, it's products, services or people. It could be as simple as a free report on a postcard or inside an email or the first thing you see when you visit their medical practice web site.

A low-risk or irresistible offer is usually something free for the prospective patient or reader of your email, web site or offline promotional piece or advertisement finds value in that elicits some call-to-action. It could be as simple as coupon, a free book, a checklist, a free DVD, etc. It's usually a free 'something' that engages and entices the reader to want to know more about who you are and what you are selling.

As a fundraising advisor for non-profits over the past decade, one of the strategies I consistently communicate to their graphic designers and leadership is 'give the reader something free and ask them for their money.' It's common sense. Just about everyone will give you their email address or call a toll-free number to get something free. If you make it easy to get 'something of value' for free, free being a clearly communicated word, people inevitably will take you up on it. Then, you know you've 'qualified' a lead and can start accumulating a clearer message to those now showing interest in your business.

Some offers are easy: "Bring this coupon in and get a free cup of coffee." But others get to be more complicated. It's difficult to sell certain products or services by simply saying, "This is what it does," and "you get $20 off." Those are offers that we refer to in the marketing world as a platitude. One example we're all familiar with is 'we provide high-quality service' or 'we've been in the business since...' Webster's Dictionary defines platitude as a remark or statement that has been used too often to be interesting or thoughtful.

Some Examples Of A Low-Risk Offer Are:

- Exam, X-Rays, and Teeth Cleaning -- $150 Adults -- $100 Kids! That's a 50% Discount!
- Free 3-Dimensional, Full Mouth X-Ray and Dental Implant Exam – A $435 Value.
- Claim Your $59 Dental Exam Today!
- Download this FREE Report Today! Unleash Your Web Site and get more qualified patients!
- Fitness Center – Claim Your 7-Day Free Pass! Submit email to claim today!
- Free Retirement Goals Checklist – Start planning for your retirement today…!
- Lawyer – Free Bankruptcy Checklist – Submit Email Now …!
- Mattress Retailer – Free $75 OFF Coupon.
- Mortgage Group – FREE REPORT – The 7 Absolute MUST KNOW ITEMS Before You Buy A Home In 2012.
- Oral Surgeon – Spring Special -- $199 Oral Exam
- Painting Company – New customers only – Get 2 Rooms for $295 (Including Paint …!!!)
- Pool and Spa Service Company – Get A Free Month of Pool or Spa Cleaning.
- Realtor – 10 FREE Tips on Buying and Selling Your Home.

- Realtor – 28 Essential Tips Every Buyer Needs to know … click here!
- Free Trial Offer! 100 Square Feet of Carpet Cleaning – No Charge, No Obligation. Refer a Friend And Get Your Carpet Cleaned Next Week!
- This Free Report changes everything; Learn why your insurance may not be working for you!
- Exam, X-Rays and Flu Shot – $150 Adults - $100 Kids!
- Enter Your Name and Email Address for a Special coupon and FREE ALLERGY CHECKLIST
- Spring Special! $250 Off 6 and 12-Month Memberships
- Get Your Fourth Month FREE!
- $250 off, $350 senior citizens/U.S. Military Personnel discount
- Free Physician Consultation and Body Fat Analysis (a $500 Value!), FREE!

Each of the above low-risk offers are examples to be used as a reference. You should consult your marketing team and possibly your attorney if you believe any offer you develop may not be in accordance with local or state laws. It's also important to note that your low-risk offer needs to be tailored to your business specifically and your targeted local audience.

A **Lead Generating Web Site** Vs. A **Brochure Web Site.**

The Internet gives you an audience with nearly immediate national and international feedback and having a web site that operates as a lead-acquiring machine verses a billboard for your practice is critical to your success in digital marketing. There are generally two types of web site designs being constructed these days. It's important to understand the difference between the two when considering building or re-designing your current site...especially if you are interested in a positive return on your investment.

The two types of web sites are a **Brochure Web Site** and a **Marketing Web Site**. Now the common misconception is assuming by having a web site at all is that it qualifies as part of your marketing efforts. That is simply not the case and is important to understand as it applies to the fundamental principle differences between marketing and advertising.

The Brochure Web Site.

A Brochure Web Site's primary function is to simply educate the visitor [i.e. prospective patient] on the services, products and history of your business. Or, sometimes provide resources exclusively for the purpose of branding. We call it a brochure web site because it is really no more than a glorified electronic version of your business brochure.

While brochure web sites can play a role in your business to verify your business's existence for a-would-be prospective customer, there should be little expectation that it will be a significant part of your overall marketing. For the overall positioning is about the company itself and not on the prospective customers' needs nor provides a compelling reason [i.e. Low-Risk Offer] for that visitor to take an action which is at the heart of a "Marketing Web Site."

MARKETING TIP # 214

Be sure that on your web site you have pictures of the outside of your office. You'd be surprised how many times patients get lost and drive right by a doctor's office. The more information you can give them to help relieve the stress of visiting the doctor's office, the better. It's also helpful to have nice pictures of your staff also. Make your patients feel as comfortable as possible.

The Lead Generating Web Site.

A Lead Generating Web Site has one mission that IS critical to your business. That is to attract interested visitors to your site and convert/qualify them as prospects to create the opportunity for more future customers.

The Lead Generating Web Site is all about having the visitor take a specific action that you decide upon. It can involve signing up for an event, calling a number or entering information such as name and email in exchange for: an informational article or newsletter, CD, DVD, checklist, free report or video of value and substance that has relevant information of interest to the prospective patient. That is essential to the overall strategy and Value Ladder in order to grow your business.

Remember, the ultimate goal of a marketing web site is to generate and qualify new leads and business opportunities for the online success of your business. As businesses begin to look at their web sites more analytically, most will find they have brochure web sites not marketing web sites. The question you should ask yourself if you don't have a web site at all is...'do you want a brochure website or one that generates more customers and makes you money...or both?'

Follow Up Is Critical To Success.

What good are new leads or new prospective customers to your business if you never call, email or send them information about your business? Everyone wants to communicate differently these days. And, if you have followed the Principles outlined here, you will soon find that 'The Fortune Is In The Follow-Up!'

For example, if you have someone who visits your "Lead Generating Web Site" and you've clearly communicated your low-risk offer to them, they in turn, are beginning to know, like and trust you. Soon, with the appropriate follow-up and strategic use of your value scale messages, you will be able to turn these prospective customers into paying customers. But, it's critical to understand that not everyone likes to be communicated with in the same way. Therefore, having a strong auto-generated email program in place to email your growing list is important. Having a strong Facebook Business Page with regular, daily posts is also important. Some people like receiving special offers via SMS text messages.

The important thing to remember is that when you begin to follow-up with these people over and over again and you are consistently showing them value via the strategic low-risk offers or information you've developed, they will begin to find value in you and your business too!

MARKETING TIP #4,163:

"When your prospect sees you in multiple places online, you are perceived to be the expert. They will begin to feel like they have spent lots of time with you. This allows them to trust you and spend lots of money with you."

CHAPTER 8

Handling Social Media and Managing Your Online Reputation.

Don't be afraid of negative comments. Build up a nice positive culture. From time to time you'll receive negative comments, but deal with it in the moment promptly and courteously, and give people the benefit of the doubt.

My professional opinion and that of other marketing and PR professionals and healthcare strategists is that when you receive a negative comment out in public, that that's a great opportunity to demonstrate stellar customer service right out in the open. Turn the situation around. Act promptly and you could very well end up having a patient for life, and having many, many people observe the wonderful attention that you gave the situation is powerful 'word of mouth marketing.'

Believe it or not, fear actually stops a lot of doctors dead in their tracks. Fear of making a mistake and spending too much money for something. Fear of managing your reputation online, being exposed on social media or having your practice become invaded with too many phone calls and patient inquiries. Well, guess what?

Did you know the number one fear that stops doctors from building a really significant brand or presence on

Facebook is fear of negative comments? Can you believe that? Physicians will not even set up a Fan Page.

There are entire books dedicated to both sides of the argument … 'The Ten Reasons Why Doctors Should Avoid Social Media' or 'Why Every Doctor Needs To Be On Facebook.' The way you should really be looking at it is … if your patients are there, you should be to!

One other important note I'd like to mention on the topic of Facebook. Social Media mogul, Gary Vaynerchuk calls social media "word of mouth marketing on steroids," and of course Facebook is the number one social network. Facebook marketing expert Mari Smith and her team are very excited about all of these different sites working together to qualify and generate new prospective leads and inquiries for businesses today. Mari notes, "Facebook is leading the way but social media inserted into your overall marketing budget and strategy is so important moving forward. Social media is creating massive shifts and changing the way we 'do' marketing. "

MARKETING TIP # 545

It's recommended by physicians and social media teams that manage the Facebook pages and profiles of health practitioners that you post one to two times per day. There's nothing worse than a prospective patient finding your Facebook Page and seeing that you haven't posted or updated the Timeline in 6 months or even worse, years. Posting one to two times per day is helpful for your SEO (Search Engine Optimization). Most people might miss your post, BUT, don't measure your Facebook productivity by engagement with others at your page/profile. You should be more concerned about reach versus engagement – meaning how many people did your various posts 'reach' – not how many "Liked" it or commented on a post you made.

I want you to know that you don't need to be intimidated by all the different too many phone calls, reputation management profile sites like HealthyGrades.com or Vitals.com, and don't avoid social media platforms. If you believe everything your colleagues tell you about marketing – think about how successful they really are right now at this moment.

You don't need 27 thousand fans. You don't even need 2,700 fans. There are plenty of successful medical clinics and primary care offices that have small 80-250 Facebook fan pages. What if you only had 500 or 5,000 genuine fans on Facebook or Google+ or Twitter? When they engage, they love you, they in turn, spread and share their love for your business or brand with their friends. And what if you could create that in 100 Days?

Have A Social Media Marketing Strategy In Addition To An "Offline" Marketing Plan

The key to generating ROI from your social media marketing is by making the most of the time that you contribute to these activities. The way to make the most of your time is to have a plan or a strategy.

Your Media Mix Should Also Include "Social Media"

Based on the research and information gathered about current and potential followers and customers, set up or expand your social media accounts. This may mean creating a Facebook business page and/or group, a LinkedIn company page or group, a YouTube channel or a Flickr account for photos. Twitter, Google+, Stumbleupon, Tumblr and other accounts may be part of this initial effort as well. Each site has its advantages, and each has strategies for its use.

Currently, Facebook remains dominant in many categories including time spent on any U.S. website according to the NM Incite – the numbers are truly staggering to look at. Facebook visitors spent over 53.5 billion total minutes on their site in 2010 according to the Neilson, Netview, Home and Work (May 2011) study of the Top 10 Web Brands.

The 20 Minute Rule Of Social Media Engagement: Morning, Noon And Night.

I recently learned that one of the greatest software and computer developers said early on in his career (and I'm paraphrasing), that the person who creates 'online communities' over the Internet will make millions. While this computer designer missed his opportunity to create one of the largest online communities in the world, how true does that statement ring with us today? Our entire online world is all about community these days isn't it?

MARKETING TIP #963:

"Pharmaceutical Representatives want your business, but they need to earn it. Talk to them. Ask them about your colleagues and if they have practitioners that are doing unique things in the community. Ask your Reps to send you referrals/leads. They want to earn your business and this is a great way to do it! You can learn a lot about your competition by simply talking to your Pharmaceutical Reps."

According to a recent info-graphic I studied recently each Facebook user spends on average 15 hours and 33 minutes a month on the site. As a marketing professional whose job it is to spend time and money on these sites, I certainly enjoy these online communities and lose track of time -- until I started applying a personal sixty-minute rule to my daily marketing activities.

Yes, it's true. I am the first to agree that it's hard to escape the allure of looking up old friends on Facebook, watching the latest movie trailer on YouTube, RT-ing on Twitter, Digg-'n stuff and Meeting Up with like-minded colleagues on MeetUp. These addictive, enticing and tempting platforms must not distract us from our purpose which is to engage our fans and followers and be "social" in a way that spurs conversation and dialogue with those people who know, like and trust us and our business.

It's no secret that social media is a disruptive force in marketing for business professionals in this modern day of technological innovation and relationally-challenged age. Social media has changed the world of marketing for years to come. Just imagine if the printing press, radio, television, the brochure, the business card, newspapers and bill boards were all invented and released to the public all at the same time. That would be a lot for any one business to capture effectively. Essentially, that significant learning curve and workload was released to marketers and businesses because of social media just in the past few years.

But after spending hundreds (if not thousands) of hours inside the time sucking bubble of these alluring socially-centered sites, I can tell you it is absolutely possible to manage and navigate your entire business and marketing presence in sixty minutes a day.

I'm convinced that those who learn to manage their time better and be more productive will be the Marketers in social media marketing that will excel to the level of experts in their profession. Yes, Marketers like myself spend enormous amounts of time managing our online presence -- but that's our job. We're supposed to be online updating our various Pages, Channels and Twitter feeds.

Now, with the advent of social media dashboards or online command centers my daily logins and work in social media has changed dramatically in the past few years.

Create Your Profiles And Then Start Controlling And Managing Your Profiles.

Once your profiles are designed, updated with the appropriate marketing detail, and you become experienced with engaging, posting, and sharing content on each of the platforms you've chosen that are most pertinent to your business and target audience, you can do social media in 60 minutes a day.

Why Are Social Media Dashboards Important?

- Dashboards allow you to manage multiple social profiles
- Dashboards allow you to track your brand mentions
- Dashboards allow you to analyze social media fans, followers and obtain detailed traffic analyses
- Dashboards allow you to see the bulk of your profiles on one screen
- Dashboards allow you to schedule posts days, weeks and months in advance across multiple social media profiles and sites.
- Dashboards allow you to engage from one place as opposed to several individual platforms.
- If you don't currently use a dashboard for the majority of your activity, it will absolutely change your perspective on and engagement in social media. Dashboards eliminate the need to log into several social media platforms and you can stop toggling between screens -- all of which will be a big time-saver. Trust me; I'm speaking from experience here.

Explore Your Options And Choose The Right Dashboard That Works For You.

There are plenty of options to choose from. You can choose Hootsuite, TweetDeck, Sprout Social, Ping.fm, NetVibes, MarketMeSuite, Jungle Torch, Trackur and more. There's too many to list, but explore some of them. Most have free accounts or trial periods that allow you to really choose the one that works best for you.

MARKETING TIP #324

"The Goal of Any Online Marketing Program Is To Create Online Sign Posts In The Places Where Your Customers Travel To On The Internet As Possible And Then Direct That Traffic Towards Your Web Site."

Constructing Your Facebook Signpost.

The top three reasons why business owners use Facebook, aside from the 1 billion plus members it recently acquired (October 2013), is the following:

- Build connections for your business and develop long-lasting relationships with your current customers. Did you know that Facebook has more than 1 billion users worldwide? (Nielsen US Data, October 2012)
- Engage your current customers in a two-way conversation and encourage them to like and share your Page posts. Did you know that over 3.2 billion posts on Facebook are liked and commented on *daily*?
- Facebook is the modern form of 'word-of-mouth' marketing to get sales for your business. Approximately 80% of consumers said that they are more likely to try new things based on friends' suggestions made in social media. (Nielsen US Data, October 2012)
- Facebook might seem like a 'Mom' site or a place online that college kids and teenagers go to share photos. While it is all of these things, it is so much more. If you put in just a little effort, you too can boost your Facebook interactions by 10, 20, even 30 percent or more in just weeks. Done right, you can yield a wealth of new information, fans, and customers who will spend real money as a result of your diligence.

The Difference Between A Profile, Group And Page.
A Facebook Profile & Timeline

This is where it all starts when you join Facebook. A Facebook Profile is accompanied by a 'timeline' is where you can update your personal information. Your profile and timeline is accompanied by how much or little you want to share. Job title, place of business, address, headshot photos, family pictures, etc. It's really the first place people start when they join Facebook.

Profiles are electronic whiteboards of your personal life and personal information. Business owners cannot create Business 'Pages' or 'Groups' without having and creating a personal profile on Facebook.com.

A Facebook Group

According to HubSpot.com, a Facebook 'Group' is a unique community on Facebook organized around a common interest. Any Facebook user can create a group, such as the "Social Marketing Signposts Book Club." The people in this unique list are committed to talking about, discussing and chatting about this particular book. Group members can engage in 'LIVE' group chats and can receive email style notifications. You can create a Facebook Group for your business by visiting Facebook.com/groups.

A Facebook Page

Similar to your website homepage for your business, your Facebook Page is your Facebook Business Homepage. Similar to Groups, anyone can join, share and like your information when seen. You can create a Facebook Page for your business by visiting Facebook.com/pages.

Steps To Help You Get Started:

Spend a little time researching your competitors. Go to Facebook.com/search. Look at how often your competitors are posting. What time(s) of day are the posting? What are they posting? Pictures? Videos? Articles? News links? Questions? Take note on these posts how many people 'are talking about this. Here are some general rules ...

- Post every day. It may seem like a lot but as people visit more frequently each day, they will see your posts in their newsfeed. If you are only posting once or twice a week – there are now studies that show this is a 'turn-off' for prospective customers. It essentially says 'if they posted one last week and three times last month ... chances are their customer service is lousy.'
- Posting 3 to 5 times each day can be good for a large majority of business pages.
- Focus on engagement. You are trying to connect and get a response from your community. As questions, post articles, links, tips, recipes, etc.
- Use Calls-to-Action. On occasion, not every time, probably once every 5 or 6 posts, tell people to "Like"

or comment on a post you made. Or, have them watch a video you recently made at your web site.

- If you decide to post five times a week, one of the posts should be a sales message and four posts should have helpful or fun content for your community.
- Make sure you post lots and lots of photos. People love photos and research has shown that pictures consistently get more "likes" and engagement from community members and fans when used in status updates for Business Pages.

"I love mobile marketing because it's so fast and easy to engage with a brand on my smart phone and tablet. One marketing tool we suggest physicians and their staff take advantage of is check-ins on Facebook and SMS (Short Message Service, that's texting). Every person that walks into your business or is even in the vicinity of your office could pick you up on their GPS or smart phone. They're a hot prospect for you. Even if you have a business based out of your home and you provide mainly home visits to your customers, you've got tons and tons of ways that you can draw people (i.e. prospective patients) in to get more engagement with your business and brand in social media."

Michael Tetreault | January 2014 | Atlanta, GA

I know it's very, very noisy out there so how do you stand out? How do you reach your target audience without wasting a lot of time sitting in front of your computer for hours on end with chatting, friending and liking?

Research tells us that fear actually stops a lot of people. Fear of making a mistake on Facebook. Fear of being exposed or having your privacy invaded and the like. And guess what? Did you know the number one fear that stops businesses from building a really significant brand or presence on Facebook is fear of negative comments? Can you believe that? Businesses will not even set up a Fan Page.

My personal experience and that of other social media and branding strategists is that when you receive a negative comment out in public, that that's a great opportunity to demonstrate stellar customer service right out in the open. Turn the situation around. Act promptly and you could very well end up having a patient for life, and having many, many people observe the wonderful attention that you gave the situation is powerful 'word of mouth marketing.'

Don't be afraid of negative comments. Build up a nice positive culture. From time to time you'll receive negative comments, but deal with it in the moment promptly and courteously, and give people the benefit of the doubt.

One other important note I'd like to mention on the topic of Facebook. Social Media mogul, Gary Vaynerchuk calls social media "word of mouth marketing on steroids," and of course Facebook is the number one social network.

Facebook marketing expert Mari Smith and her team gets very excited about is all of these different sites working together qualify and generate new prospective patient leads and inquiries for physicians. Mari continues to note, "Facebook is leading the way but social media inserted into your overall marketing budget and strategy is so important moving forward. Social media is creating massive shifts and changing the way we 'do' marketing."

There is really no "right" way to do everything on Facebook, but following these general rules or guidelines will help get you started.

Essential Components Of A Social Media Marketing Plan

- **Summary of Current Situation**
  Should include the following areas: Positioning; Area Statistics & Demographics; Market Segmentation; Methods of Market Segmentation; and Target Audience Identification & Analysis.

- **Competitive Analysis**
  Should include the following areas: Competitive Service Analysis; Competitive Fees & Pricing; Internal Marketing Strategy; Company Name, Logo & Byline; Service Quality, Market Research; Supporting

Surveys; Customer Care & Internal Marketing
Analysis/Situational Report(s).

- **Current Influence In Social Media**
  Should include the following areas: Online Reviews;
  Online Competitive Service Listing Analysis; Google
  Presence; Facebook Report Card; Web Site Analysis
  and Report Card; Recommended SEO Keyword(s);
  and Social Media
  Statistical Reports.

- **Recommended Advertising & Promotion Strategy**
  Should include the following areas: Proposed Budget
  & Advertising Objectives; Current Marketplace Facts
  You Should Be Aware of; Recommended Advertising
  & Promotional Strategies; Upcoming 12-Month
  Goals; Recommended Marketing Tools To Be Used
  Over the Next 12-Months; Recommended "Offline"
  Marketing and Promotional Strategy; Recommended
  "Online" Marketing and Promotional Strategy.

BONUS
MATERIALS

MERRY MARKETING:
4 Ways To Fire Up Your Holiday Promotions

'Tis the season to drape your signage and office lobby in greenery, twinkling lights, hang a "LIVE" Christmas wreath onto your door and get prepped for the onset of happy holiday patients.

Busy patients are out and about and rushing to get their last minute shopping done and more importantly, fill those last-minute prescriptions and forgotten office visits before the end of the year. That's where you come in. The holiday season is an ideal opportunity for you to soften the beaches in their minds that your medical practice is the best spot to stop and refuel and make sure your holiday season is a healthy one. It's also a time to draw their attention to refilling upcoming prescriptions, book January appointments about nutritional and healthy eating seminars you're planning to do in your office and tell them about a special holiday themed event or promotion your running.

With an ounce of creativity, your holiday event or promotion can be as simple as dropping a holiday prescription reminder in the mail to each of your patients or tell them that a donation point for a local charity or that you're accepting canned goods for a holiday charity drive. The key is creating enough top of mind awareness to keep your medical practice on speed dial during a time when patients are so easily distracted.

Here are three great ideas for driving foot traffic to your private-pay medical during the bustling holiday season.

First, Collect Canned Goods or Host a Charity Drive.

Nothing shows goodwill during the holidays like giving to others. It's one of the easiest and most charitable efforts you can do each year and still involve your patients. It's easy to advertise, easy to collect and easy to drop off donated items once the charity drive is over.

We recommend partnering with a locally based charitable organization for a holiday collection drive. Habitat for Humanity or the Habitat Home Store (if applicable) in your area might be looking for clothing, toiletry items, hammers, etc. Local churches are always looking for partners to assist them in their community with the collection of canned goods, food and other items.

Ask your local area churches close to your practice about how you can help collect items and drop them off this holiday season. Then, send a list of these items to your patients by email, in the office via a flyer, etc. Ask for support relating to your charity drive by promoting your practice and location through social media and email.

Besides doing something good for your community, if your patients, Facebook fans or LinkedIn followers know that they can knock off to-do's on their list, fill their hubbies prescription, get a quick sore throat check-up and drop off a holiday donation, they're more likely to make a point in stopping by. Because space is an issue for medical practice owners, consider collecting smaller gifts such as pet toys for a local animal shelter or hygiene items for a homeless center and put the collection boxes, nicely decorated of course, and positioned in a prominent location where most of your patients will see items being donated in your lobby or waiting area.

Second, Use Direct Mail.

Holiday cards to your favorite patients, drug and DME suppliers and physician supporters are a great way to encourage physician referrals towards your practice in the New Year. This not only creates a personal connection but it's also an opportunity you to slip in a note about your practice, special services you provide and about your charity drive throughout the season.

Handle the mailing yourself with an on-the-go compact mailing system or stamps.com so you can get your cards in the mail pronto. If you miss the post-Christmas mailing deadline, New Year's cards work just as well to remind your followers to stop in and book their next appointment.

Third, Amp up Your Patient Testimonials, Online Reviews, Reputation and Social Media.

There's nothing better than a great patient testimonial, am I right? Well, with the holidays upon us, people, especially your patients, typically feel in a generous and giving mood. That being said, they'd probably enjoy writing a sentence or two about you, their experience with your practice and staff on one of the physician review web sites.

Finally, You Have A Facebook Page, Don't You? If Not, Get One. Now!

Facebook, Twitter, Instagram and Pinterest are thrifty and effective buzz-generating mediums for promoting just about anything, especially good word of mouth referrals. Create Facebook Events for each promotion and invite your friends. Post photos on Instagram of your holiday lights, your staff in elf hats, holiday treats, and happy patients (with their permission of course). Create a Pinterest contest where customers can pin photos of their donation they brought into your office in order to qualify to win a free gift basket. The options are endless but bottom line, social media creates a visual online picture that your medical practice is the place to be during the holiday season.

The Top 50 Web Site Design Resources.

1. CSSBeauty.com
2. CSSDrive.com
3. THEFWA.com
4. Thebestdesigns.com
5. Cssvault.com
6. Unmatchedstyle.com
7. Designmeltdown.com
8. Designshack.co.uk
9. Webcreme.com
10. Cssheaven.com
11. Cssremix.com
12. Bestwebgallery.com
13. Cssmania.com
14. Patterntap.com
15. Csselite.com
16. Cssclip.com
17. Designbombs.com
18. Siteinspire.com
19. Edustyle.net
20. Styleboost.com
21. Genuinestyle.net
22. Css-website.com
23. Cssbased.com
24. Mostinspired.com
25. Stylegala.com
26. Css-design-yorkshire.com
27. My3w.org
28. Cssimport.com
29. W3csites.com
30. Screenalicious.com
31. Cssimpress.com
32. Dark-i.com
33. Screenfluent.com
34. Designbygrid.com
35. Cssburst.com
36. Cssheroes.com
37. Inspirationking.com
38. Pulse360.com
39. Cssflavor.com
40. Csstux.com
41. Csscollection.com
42. Nicestylesheet.com
43. Dezinspiration.com
44. Cssartillery.com
45. Stylecrunch.com
46. Makebetterwebsite.com
47. Cssliquid.com
48. Cssline.com
49. Onepixelarmy.com
50. Cssdump.com

Top Performing List Companies To Help Your Medical Practice Grow In Any Economy.

- o SoloAdDirectory.com
- o ArcaMay.com
- o Townhall.com
- o Newsmax.com
- o Jaaxy.com
- o DedicatedEmails.com
- o TheHomeBusinessAgency.com
- o AdBlade.com
- o Pulse360.com

When To Use Billboard Advertising

Internet travelers drive just as fast, if not faster, than speeders on the interstate. But, if you're in business any amount of time, someone will contact you eventually asking whether or not you'd like to purchase billboard advertising in your local geography. In most cases, billboard advertising in not within the budget or area near your practice. It can be very expensive and ineffective if you don't know how to use it wisely.

With outdoor advertising upping the stakes and becoming increasingly more competitive, it's important to know how to make your advertising count. Here are a couple strategies to ensure your billboard has the highest chance of being noticed, and more importantly, remembered.

1. For Billboards, Six Words or Less is Ideal.
2. Get Noticed, But Don't Make Your Billboards a Huge Distraction.
3. Don't Say It, Show It.

The most common and best use of billboard advertising for small business, and that includes medical practices ... are using words found on interstate billboards such as "exit now." Some might say "turn right" or "turn left" or how many miles to the destination, but the point is they give directions. Never assume your audience knows what you want them to do. If you're considering billboard advertising, this is the most effective use of your money, advertising and promotion in this way.

"I am a Marriage and Family Therapist in Las Vegas, Nevada. I have had a private practice for 6 years now. Over the last few years my client load was about 25 to 30 clients that I saw per week. Last week I saw 50 clients and the week before that it was 46 and this week I have 50 scheduled again! My email and telephone have been lighting with people asking for my services. You will not be disappointed. Your business will grow like never before."

~Marriage Therapist | Las Vegas, NV

"We had dabbled with SEO but couldn't get much traction. We saw some drastic results in one of our markets – San Diego. We got to page 1 and even number 1 for a few of our top keywords. I'm impressed."

~The Local Hearing Clinic | San Diego, CA

"Michael is an expert marketing strategist for businesses and nonprofits who is excellent in the areas of brand development, messaging and push strategies. His knowledge of current and emerging social media platforms is extensive."

~Attorney | Atlanta, GA

"I'd suggest everyone read the section on the low-risk offer to find out how to say things to your patient's right from the start -- a strategy I see a lot of doctors miss entirely. The later chapters tell you things you can do to provide focus and clarity for staff
who might work for you."

~Internal Medicine Physician | California

THE MARKETING MD

What Still Works To Attract New Patients.
Plus What To Do When You Run Out Of Ideas.
+
Delivering the right message, to the right patient,
at the right time, makes every patient,
the best patient.

By Michael Tetreault

Elite MD, Inc. | Elite MD Publishing
4080 McGinnis Ferry Road
Building 800, Suite 801
Alpharetta, GA 30005

itemize it
thus

Dr Rastashari ?

Mike Bohrer   390-0600

Garry +

URGENT COST MORE
PERSONALLY (out / pocket)
DRIVES UP PREMIUMS
(will pay more in
long run)

p28
33
3
96

Millennium

* read Sonvuss contract
How much
Do they ✓ <u>are</u> daily

NOT Hosp. based → low deductible

< deductible

< credit card.

Paying extra to use Urgent Care

RE-NEGOTIATE → Abby Blair
NOW Horizon rep

— United Horm Care Community.
(medicaid product)
AmeriHealth value Network

— Bus Co's

— NJ transit
Greyhound plesinkulla

Made in the USA
Lexington, KY
11 June 2015